BUCKSKIN

AND

SPURS

BUCKSKIN

AND

SPURS

A GALLERY OF FRONTIER
ROGUES AND HEROES

BY

GLENN SHIRLEY

HASTINGS HOUSE, PUBLISHERS

NEW YORK

For permission to republish certain of the chapters included in this book, the author wishes to thank STANDARD MAGAZINES, INC., STADIUM PUBLISHING CORPORATION, and ALMAT PUBLISHING CORPORATION of New York; WESTERN PUBLICATIONS of Austin, Texas; and MODERN MAN of Skokie, Illinois.

Published simultaneously in Canada
by S. J. Reginald Saunders, Publishers,
Toronto 2B.

Library of Congress Catalog Card Number: 58-8280

Printed in the United States of America

For
CARRIE
KENNETH
and
GLENDA LEA

Contents

Illustrations

Foreword

IN my wide research into the history and lore of our American West I have collected many unusual and dramatic tales of little written-about events and people. Some have been mentioned in books and journals, but their stories have not been set down as a whole. In most cases the parts they played in our Western frontier development are not sufficient to warrant full biographical study. Some of them existed for too short a period.

My first book, *Toughest of Them All,* recounted the lives of some of these characters, and this new volume adds a dozen more. The stories cover a wide range of material, including the unique capture of a notorious Arizona murderer, the exploits of the man who invented bulldogging, and the activities of the West's most talented bank robber.

Taken from authentic sources, this is a fact book on more "toughs," bad and good—some in buckskin, some with spurs.

GLENN SHIRLEY

STILLWATER, OKLAHOMA.

BUCKSKIN

AND

SPURS

1. Burton C. Mossman

The Ranger and the Apache Devil

CAP MOSSMAN, who had already accounted for so many criminals-at-large in the Arizona Territory, was determined to wind up his law-enforcement career with the final elimination of Augustin Chacon, the gaunt, be-whiskered bandit who for years had been terrorizing the southwestern border country.

Both men had become almost legendary figures. Chacon, a big man, with long, gorilla arms and huge paws at the ends of them, was the killingest outlaw ever to run loose in the wild border country of the Territory. He exceeded Billy the Kid in the number to die by his gun. His score totalled twenty-nine. And he was a killer who shot men down with no more compassion than other people would kill a rattlesnake. He was a half-breed Apache, but was inspired by no idealistic drive to avenge the wrongs of his Indian blood-brothers. Unlike the great Indian chieftains, he was just a ruthless bandit. Yet, for all his admixture of white blood, he was as stealthy and deadly as Geronimo himself.

The Mexicans sang of him in their long *canciones* as a man who robbed the rich and gave to the poor, but he was nothing but a thief and murderer. Yet he had a sweetheart in almost every mining camp, and his many Spanish-speaking sympathizers, believing he was persecuted because he had the courage to fight against the conquering *Americanos* who had taken over the land and become wealthy in the process, protected him. With a huge gang of Mexicans, he would cross the border and raid some Arizona ranch house or store, murder the victims and all the witnesses, load his pack animals with plunder and leisurely return to Mexico.

The law had him only once. In 1896, he looted a store at Morenci and butchered the storekeeper. Sheriff Billy Birchfield, of Graham County, led a posse after him. Deputy Sheriff Davis tracked the bandit, following bloodstains, to the hut of a Mexican named Contreras. Here there ensued a fight in which Chacon, after killing his old friend Salcido, a deputy, while the latter was urging the bandits to surrender, was himself wounded. Finally, Chacon was captured in a box canyon and brought in to Solomonville, where he was tried and sentenced to be hung. The sentence was appealed, but the Supreme Court refused to change the verdict.

Because the authorities suspected a plot to rescue Chacon, he was removed to Tucson from the Solomonville jail. The date for the hanging was fixed anew; and the convicted man was sent back to Solomonville. A petition was circulated asking for a milder penalty for Chacon, but the governor turned it down flat. However, with the help of a pretty girl from nearby Morenci, who smuggled him some hacksaw

"Cap" Burton C. Mossman of the Arizona Rangers, captor of notorious bandit, Augustin Chacon. *Courtesy* Frontier Fix, *Ed. Bartholomew, Houston, Texas.*

blades hidden in a prayer book, he escaped jail, hid out in the Sierra Madres of Mexico, and resumed his forays across the border with increased savagery.

He pursued his bloody course for several years, through the cactus and chaparral stretches of the Southwest. He crossed and recrossed the border so many times he once sent word to Cochise County's famous sheriff, John Slaughter, that he was coming to Tombstone to get him. Slaughter cut loose on the bandit with a shotgun, and might have killed him had not Chacon reached the edge of a gully and ducked from sight in time to miss the hail of lead.

Another time he killed two prospectors in Eagle Canyon, near Solomonville, where he was under sentence of death, stole a horse, and with a .45-70 rifle, also a part of the loot, kept his pursuers at a distance as he fled west. At New River, near Phoenix, he raided a sheep camp, killing two Americans, robbed the stage at Agua Fria, then rode south into the Papago country, playing hide-and-seek with sheriff's posses for two weeks before he vanished.

Eventually he became a fabulous figure in song and story, like Murieta in California, the Younger brothers and James boys of Missouri, and the Daltons of Oklahoma, and was accused of most of the unsolved crimes in the territory. He grew a bushy black beard to conceal his identity, and the Mexicans called him *Peludo,* the Hairy One. At the zenith of his blood-dripped career, a steely, jut-jawed cowpuncher named Burton C. Mossman rode into Arizona.

Mossman grew up in the rough Territory of New Mexico. He had "cut his teeth on his daddy's six-shooter" fighting cattle rustlers and sheepmen. At an early age, he learned to cuss in two languages, tend his own business, read sign like an Apache, and play a good game of poker.

At twenty-one he was ramrod of a New Mexico ranch running 8,000 cattle. At twenty-seven, he was manager of the Bloody Basin outfit of northern Arizona, where he accomplished the almost impossible feat of gathering 10,000 cattle from a country too rough for a pack animal. Three years later, he was called to manage the Hash Knife, the most famous of the cow outfits of old Arizona, with two million acres and 60,000 head on the Little Colorado River, and the reputation of being the biggest bunch of killers and thieves in the Territory. Its own cowboys were stealing it blind before Mossman became superintendent.

Mossman selected a few men he could trust, taught them the rudiments of rangeland detective work, and within two years had run the rustler bands out of the country, sent them to prison, or extinguished them. He had a reputation as the best man hunter in Arizona when the Rangers were organized in 1901.

This organization was the result of lawless conditions in Arizona at the turn of the century. Nervy little John Slaughter had sort of "pacified" things down in the southeastern corner of the Territory. But after he quit the sheriff's office and retired to his San Bernardino rancho near Douglas, the badmen had drifted in again. All along the Mexican line from Yuma to New Mexico, where miles of mesquite were covered with unprotected cattle, rustlers and horse thieves had "run their own brand on the range." Up across Grand Canyon to the north stolen stock was run over into Utah and Colorado. No one had made this part of the Territory hot enough to discourage thieves and killers, and it had become a haven for outlaws of every description and color.

It looked like the small cattlemen would have to quit. The big outfits such as Slaughter, the Erie Cattle Company, the

C.C.C., and Colonel Bill Greene hired armies of fighting men to protect their interests, but they weren't making the rustlers hard to catch.

The sheriffs and their deputies were practically of no help at all. Many were cattle thieves themselves, or had been. Even when they tried, the rustlers would scatter to the four winds and fade like Apache hostiles.

These were ideal conditions for Augustin Chacon. His depredations and those of men like him were running out capital and settlers. Something had to be done, or "give the thieves a bill of sale to the Territory." When the legislature met in March, they authorized the governor to create a body of men to bring law and order to the country, and Governor Nathan O. Murphy asked Mossman to form a Ranger company.

The job paid only a hundred and twenty a month, less than some cowboys were making at the Hash Knife. Mossman's head bookkeeper drew a hundred and twenty-five. But Mossman didn't consider the pay. Six peace officers in six months had been slain, and not one of their killers had been caught. It was a tough country. Someone had to clean it up. Mossman had proved that he was qualified. He felt a duty to Arizona, and had to perform it before he could return to horses and cattle—the life he loved.

He was appointed captain and thereafter became known as "Cap" Mossman. They gave him only thirteen men—one sergeant and twelve privates—but they went to work. They ranged the great southwestern territory and became as much a part of it as its deserts and hills and valleys. No Northwest Mounted Police, Texas Rangers, or other famous crew of hard-riding, straight-shooting, fearless men ever did more for civilization.

There were only fourteen of them, covering an area larger than New England, but they did what hundreds of sheriffs and deputies had failed to do—"slam the fear of God into the whole army of the orneriest hombres who ever straddled leather." They worked swiftly, secretly. Mossman himself took Black Jack Christian's trail and ran him and his gang of killers into the White Mountains of New Mexico, and they never came back. He captured scores of others.

Stories of his prowess became legends. But the most dangerous criminal, the one he wanted to account for more than any other, the gaunt, whiskered Augustin Chacon, was still at large. The real test of his career as a law enforcement officer would be the capture of the Mexican half-breed bandit.

Governor Murphy demanded it. Territorial politicians were making a great deal of talk about it, and Cap's enemies, including sheriffs envious of his reputation, were quick to point out his failure. For every boast about Cap's success in cleaning up the Territory, someone jibed:

"What about Chacon?"

This sort of talk touched Cap on the raw. The idea of Chacon still at large hounded him like an obsession. Chacon was hiding in Mexico, and Arizona officers had no legal right to cross the border to kill or capture Mexican citizens. The privilege applied only to Americans chasing Americans and Mexicans chasing their own nationals.

How to lay hands on Chacon under these circumstances? Cap worked out a plan, risky but perhaps feasible, which would require the aid of two former law enforcement officers who had later turned outlaws, Burt Alvord and Billy Stiles. Mossman, in pursuit of his scheme, passed the word around that he would pay plenty to be put on Chacon's track. Meanwhile he talked his plan over with his friend, Judge Barnes.

The judge had at one time been a friend of Burt Alvord, an early-day Tombstone character. Alvord was short, bald-headed, and as dark as a Mexican. He was as tough as Chacon, and as notorious, except for a record of brutal murder. His chief interests were guns, horses, pool halls, poker and rustling. He had been a deputy sheriff for John Slaughter off and on, and worked on his ranch as a cowboy. He was present the night the little lawman had pumped his shotgun blast at Chacon.

Afterward, he had served as marshal in a couple of towns and rode shotgun for Wells Fargo before taking a professional interest in train robbery. He and Bob Downing—whose real name was believed to be Jackson, a former member of the Sam Bass gang in Texas—a ruffian named Matt Burts, and a snaky little gunman named Billy Stiles, robbed an express car at Cochise Station, ten miles west of Willcox, and hurried back to town to establish alibis.

The amount obtained was about thirty thousand dollars. The gang used the utmost caution, and might have gotten away scot-free had they not become so over-confident and staged another robbery at Fairbank, a few miles west of Tombstone. A member of their gang, Three-Fingered Jack Dunlap, was filled with buckshot. The posse found him next day lying beside the trail in the desert. He lived just long enough to tell the officers what they wanted to know.

Alvord, Stiles, Burts and Downing were arrested. Stiles turned state's evidence because Alvord had taken all the loot. No one else knew where he had hidden it. Wells Fargo men, anxious to recover the money, made a deal with Stiles and set him free, hoping he could help them find the hidden loot.

Stiles went to see Alvord in jail at Tombstone, but Jailer Bravin wouldn't let him in. So Billy shot Bravin, took the

Billie Stiles, of the Stiles-Alvord gang, who was used as decoy by Mossman in capture of Chacon. *Courtesy* Frontier Fix, *Ed. Bartholomew, Houston, Texas.*

Augustin Chacon, handcuffed
and chained after his capture.
Courtesy Frontier Fix, *Ed. Bartholomew, Houston, Texas.*

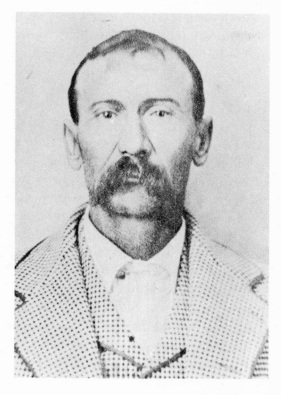

Bob Downing, member of Burt Alvord's gang and former member of Sam Bass gang in Texas. *Courtesy* Frontier Fix, *Ed. Bartholomew, Houston, Texas.*

keys off him, turned Alvord loose, and fled south with him into Sonora.

With Alvord, Stiles and Chacon all hiding across the border and wanted by the law, they surely had got acquainted. Judge Barnes suggested the possibility of contacting Chacon through Alvord.

"Of course," he added, "you may not come back all in one piece."

Cap realized his danger. But he had no quarrel with Alvord. He wanted Chacon.

Judge Barnes mentioned another point. "I know the Governor. I might be able to get him off with a light sentence if he cooperates with you. I'll give you a letter to that effect."

"All right, where is he hiding?" asked Cap.

"I couldn't say," the Judge replied. "Maybe his wife can help you. She lives in Willcox."

Cap found Alvord's wife in poor health, almost destitute, and lonely. She was willing to do anything to get her husband to give himself up and let Judge Barnes do what he could to help him. But she had no idea where he was.

She remembered that Billy Stiles had once mentioned a half brother who was a steam-pump operator in an English smelter at Minas Prietas, on the Nogalas-Guaymas railroad down in Sonora. It would be a long trip and a slim chance that he would know Alvord. Cap decided to find out, and went to Judge Barnes for the letter.

Judge Barnes put it in his own handwriting, stating the facts clearly. Alvord might even be acquitted, since nearly everybody who had seen the crime committed, was dead or had disappeared. Besides, his wife had consulted him about a divorce. He would agree to get her to postpone the matter for a while.

He gave Cap the letter, shook his hand and wished him luck.

Sheriff Dell Lewis of Cochise County and Sheriff Tom Turner of Santa Cruz told Cap he was a fool.

"We've been down to Sonora after Alvord, but got no-where—" Turner said. "Better watch out. Burt's all steamed up right now. He's liable to kill you without waiting to hear your proposition."

Meanwhile Cap was threatened with a fresh complication. A new administration, that of Theodore Roosevelt, had moved into the White House, after McKinley's assassination. Cap realized that the new people who would be appointed to office in Arizona would give him short shrift as Captain of the Rangers. He would have to work fast.

He slipped down to Nogales that night and the next morn-ing quietly boarded the train a few minutes before it left for Sonora. At Minas Prietas, he went straight to the manager of the smelter with his story. The manager thought he was crazy.

"But it ain't my head that's going to get blowed off," he said, and told Cap where to contact the half brother, who was working twenty miles back in the hills.

Cap found the half brother skeptical and surly. Cap talked fast and let the man read Judge Barnes' letter. In the end the half brother came around and fixed Cap up with a horse and saddle and gave him directions where he could find Alvord.

Cap rode for several days. One evening, as he came around a bend, he saw a hut and a stocky-built man waiting with a Winchester handy.

Cap didn't reach for his six-shooter, but rode boldly up to the man. When he was still a few yards away, the man's rifle swung level and Cap halted. Cap had never met Alvord, but he had seen his face on "wanted" placards, and knew for sure that this was the man he had so long been trying to contact.

"You're Burt Alvord," he said.

"Who the Hell's asking?"

"Cap Mossman— I guess you know who he is. But don't get riled. I haven't brought anyone with me, all this way. I've a letter to you from Judge Barnes and a message from your woman."

The rifle in the outlaw's hands wavered. But the barrels of three others, that Cap could see pointed at him from between the gaps in the wall of the hut, remained steady.

"Call off your dogs, Alvord. All I have is a revolver. I got more sense than to try to use it."

Alvord barked an order and the rifles disappeared. He now demanded to see the judge's letter.

Cap handed it over; Alvord read it slowly. He wasn't much on reading and he had to spell out the words to himself. Finally he turned again to Cap and asked how he had been able to find him.

"Billy's half brother told me," Cap replied.

"What do you want?"

"We'll get to that later," Cap told him. "Right now I'm hungry."

Alvord took him in to a supper of the usual Mexican variety. Afterward they sprawled around the fire and drank mescal. It appears that Cap's silver-and-gold-mounted Colt attracted the interest of a member of the gang.

"Let me see it," he asked.

"If you'll leave me have yours," Cap replied.

When they had traded guns, the Mexican, who had imbibed rather freely of the local poison juice, hinted: "But it would be a very pleasant thing if the next time I visit my *dulce,* I could show her this fine pistol and tell her it was a gift to me from the captain of the Arizona Rangers."

Cap replied politely: "Yes, but I am sure she would not be happy to come upon you dead on the trail somewhere. Would she now?"

For a moment murder hung in the air. But Alvord didn't want a fight just then. He had too much at stake. He ordered the bandit to hand over the fancy weapon.

Cap and Alvord had their talk later, when they could be sure no one was overhearing what they said.

Cap told Alvord: "Arrange it so I can get Chacon up near the border. If I get Chacon, you stand the chance of being acquitted, you can be with your wife again, and you and Billy Stiles can divide the reward between you, fifty-fifty."

Alvord whistled. But there were obvious risks. Chacon wouldn't fall easily into any trap they might set for him.

"Tell him," Cap suggested, "I'm a chap who's just broke out of jail and is looking for the right connections. Tell him I have a good deal all staked out. Perhaps he already knows about that pasture just across the line where Colonel Greene keeps his race horses. I don't think Chacon (tell him) could pull it off alone. Certainly I couldn't. You might add, there's a fine stallion over there Chacon might want for himself . . . It'd be a cinch for two or three working together."

Alvord thought it might work out. But he couldn't get to Chacon direct himself. Billy Stiles was the man for that. Cap realized that both Alvord and Stiles were first-rate scoundrels. But they offered him his only chance. So he decided to risk it.

Cap left next morning. Back home, things had changed as predicted. Already Teddy Roosevelt had appointed a Rough Rider, Major Brodie, territorial governor. Cap promptly submitted his resignation. Brodie wrote back, asking him to stay

Burt Alvord, go-between used by Mossman in capture of
Chacon. *Courtesy* Frontier Fix, *Ed. Bartholomew, Houston,
Texas.*

Burt Alvord (standing), at time he was deputy sheriff under
John Slaughter. *Courtesy* Frontier Fix, *Ed. Bartholomew,
Houston, Texas.*

on until he found his replacement.

This gave Cap more time. How much, he dared not even guess. The new governor might make up his mind any day. Cap hoped to get Chacon before he did. Weeks passed with no word from Alvord.

Cap contacted United States Marshal W. H. McCord at Phoenix and asked for a deputy's commission claiming that it would allow him to operate outside the Territory. McCord fell for the idea. He issued Cap his papers July 2, 1902. Cap could now fall back on his federal commission if necessary.

He had to capture Chacon. He had sworn to bring in the outlaw, and even if relieved of his office, he was going to stay on the killer's trail as long as there was even a thin hope. It was his duty to Arizona, and not until he had killed or captured the notorious bandit and brought him in to be legally hanged would he feel it completed.

And his only chance lay with those two desperate characters. Stiles was in it for half the rewards offered for Chacon. The other half didn't interest Alvord. He wanted to see his wife again, and someday dig up the loot from the Cochise robbery.

Even if they were able to lure Chacon to the border, there was no assurance Cap could take him. Chacon might kill him. But Cap vowed he wouldn't if he got the first shot.

But Cap wasn't going to kill him. It would be a greater blow to his critics if he could bring in the notorious bandit alive.

Cap received a wire from Governor Brodie. His resignation, tendered in July, would be accepted August 31st. On September 1, Tom Rynning, a former sergeant in the famous old Sixth Cavalry and lieutenant of Troop B of the Rough Riders, became the new Captain of the Rangers.

Cap was through as a Ranger. He still had his deputy United States marshal's commission. But it looked like he wouldn't even need it now.

Then the next evening, just before dark, Billy Stiles brought him word that Alvord had arranged a rendezvous with Chacon!

As Cap and Billy headed south that night and crossed into Mexico, at Naco, Cap didn't even consider that he might be riding to his death.

By morning they were a good way south of the line, near Carizzo Springs, wondering where Alvord and Chacon were. Cap was worried.

He had not been sure of Stiles' loyalty from the beginning.

But Stiles seemed disturbed over the failure to make connections as Alvord had planned. He decided they had ridden too far.

They kept out of sight in the chaparral most of the day, then started back to the border. About nine o'clock that night, somewhere east of the San José Mountains, two figures rode out into plain sight.

Alvord was being very cautious. He mentioned no names. Cap would hardly have recognized Chacon, although he had seen pictures of him, for the five years since his escape from prison had wrought a great change in him. His form was bent and his beard was tinted with gray. He was now an old man, but Cap wasn't fooled for a minute. The bandit was still as dangerous as a rattler. Alvord spoke to Chacon, who grunted non-committally. Cap began talking fast, before Chacon's suspicions would lead to a shooting. Over there, beyond the border, he said, were Colonel Greene's horses, just waiting to be run off. He threw in a remark about the stallion, too.

"We can cut the international fence," he told the bandit,

"grab them tonight, and by morning be away into Mexico again."

Chacon said little. But he remarked in Spanish that it wasn't possible. You couldn't manage unless there was more light to see by. Obviously, he suspected a trap and was choosing his own time. Cap saw he couldn't rush matters. So he proposed waiting for daylight.

They camped hidden away in the brush. They stretched out around the fire, and the long night's vigil began.

Cap fought off sleep. He intended to be alive in the morning. He kept double watch on Alvord and Stiles. He couldn't trust either of them, and any moment Chacon might try to kill him.

A dreary drizzle set in about midnight; Cap slipped into his slicker. While so doing he managed, without it being noticed by his companions, to get his revolver where he could use it fast when needed.

As dawn grayed the sky Alvord saddled his horse and said he was going to look for a spring for a drink. As he passed close to Mossman, he whispered: "Look out for Billy Stiles. He'll double-cross you." Then he mounted and was gone.

Cap knew Alvord had quit—wouldn't be back. Cap was with Chacon where he could capture him—if he was lucky. It was up to him, Mossman, now. Alvord wanted to be miles away when the showdown came.

Cap moved into position to watch both Chacon and Stiles.

They cooked something over the embers of last night's fire for breakfast. Stiles wielded the frying pan. Alvord's excuse for leaving had not satisfied Chacon. His eyes never left Mossman's face while the bacon was sizzling.

Chacon squatted by Stiles, and the two men lighted cigarettes. Cap strolled over and asked Chacon for a smoke.

Chacon obliged.

Sitting down, the outlaw was at a disadvantage; he couldn't draw quickly, but the light of a sort of intuitive awareness was in his eyes. Cap picked up a burning twig and lighted his cigarette. For a moment, because Cap's hand seemed busy, the bandit relaxed. Cap leaned down as if to shove the glowing twig back into the embers. Then he suddenly came up with his Colt.

"All right, Chacon," he shouted, "get 'em up or I'll cut you in two!"

Chacon hesitated for the fraction of a second, probably glancing hopefully in Stiles' direction. Cap shifted to cover both men. He had never taken such a chance in his life, and he never knew which side Stiles was on until the little gunman stepped over and disarmed the big outlaw. Had Chacon called Cap's bluff, Stiles would have probably helped him kill the ranger.

Cap pulled a pair of handcuffs from the lining of his coat and ordered Stiles to put them on the outlaw, Chacon. Then he backed to where his rifle was leaning against a mesquite tree, jerked the gun open and pushed a cartridge into the chamber, and leveled the weapon at his captive. He was ready for any emergency now.

"Now you, Billy, drop your own gun!" he ordered.

Billy played it innocent.

"What the hell, Cap," he protested.

Cap repeated: "Drop it, Billy!"

Billy obeyed. Cap ordered them to back away from their weapons.

"We'll leave them here," he said. "Saddle the horses, Billy; we've a long way to ride."

The little procession started off slowly toward the border,

with Stiles leading Chacon's mount. The outlaw rode with his hands cuffed behind so he could not touch the reins. Cap brought up the rear, his rifle and six-shooter ready for action. He didn't breathe easy until he had cut the border fence six miles west of Naco, and ridden through. When he saw a train coming along, he signalled it. He ordered Stiles to ride over to Bisbee with the horses. Then he boarded the train with his prisoner. This was near Packard, a little station a mile or so above the border, near Colonel Greene's pastures.

"Well, I'll be damned!" exclaimed Jim Parks, the new sheriff of Graham County, when he saw Cap climb off the local with Chacon in handcuffs.

He knew how dangerous the outlaw was, and the first thing he did was hand Cap his pistol before he stooped to clamp leg irons on the prisoner and slip new cuffs on his wrists before removing Cap's old ones.

Chacon was promptly arraigned as an escaped criminal under sentence of death. On November 21, a little more than two months later, he was led out onto the gallows. He delivered himself of a long harangue in which he maintained he was innocent of the crime for which he was being executed. To the end he remained imperturbably cheerful. At the very last moment he rolled a cigarette and smoked it calmly. As the cap was being adjusted, he shouted: "*Adios Todos Amigos!*"

That day Cap was with Colonel Greene at the Waldorf in New York. He had finished his duty to Arizona, but he had kidnapped a Mexican citizen. He feared international complications. Colonel Greene had been wanting Cap to pay him a visit, and Cap decided there was no better time to make himself scarce.

But things worked out all right for Cap Mossman. Burt

Alvord went to Canada, then to Central America, and was never heard from again. Stiles, the only other witness, was killed in a gambling casino in Nevada. Cap had several thousand dollars in the bank at Bisbee. He drew out a thousand, transferred the balance to a bank in Colorado, and went back to ranching in New Mexico.

He spent his last days at Roswell in his seven-bedroom home. Eighty-nine and confined to a wheel chair before his death, he enjoyed swapping yarns about the old times, mostly about the humorous happenings in his life.

"I never wanted to kill a man," he said.

Although he early severed all contacts with Arizona, to him belongs the credit for organizing the state's first Rangers and the respect of all honest men for carrying the law into the desert and mesquite with a fearlessness unequaled by any officer of the old Southwest.

2. George W. Pike

Remarkable Horse Thief

GEORGE W. PIKE, who spent the latter part of his life as a respected citizen of Douglas, Wyoming, was incomparably the best horse thief the West ever produced.

Where he came from originally is not known, but Western lore and range gossip have it that when he dropped off a train at Antelope in 1885, he was about thirty years old. And already he apparently had acquired the background for what was to come.

At that time Wyoming Territory was suffering from growing pains. The Fremont, Elkhorn, and Missouri Valley Railroad was building a track up the Platte to provide shipping points for cattle from the central plains of Wyoming. Previously it had been necessary to drive the herds to the Northern Pacific Railway in Montana, or to the Union Pacific in the south.

All kinds of settlements had sprung up in advance of the

railroad construction. Townsite companies had been organized in anticipation of great profits to be made in the sale of real estate with the coming of the tracks.

The town of Antelope was such a settlement. The day George Pike got off the train there the town boasted of more than three hundred inhabitants and the wildest entertainment to be found anywhere along the line. It was a single street of tents for business establishments, and small shacks in the rear of them for homes. In one of these shacks George Pike took up residence.

There was nothing in his personal appearance to bring special attention to the man. He was of medium weight and build, with dark complexion and hair. But he had a ready smile, and this quickly won him friends, just as a wildness in his blood attracted him like a magnet to the sporting element. He became an inveterate gambler.

And it was one night when he rode a hundred and seventy-five miles to play poker—and lost everything he had—that he launched on his career that was to bring him recognition as the most unique character in Wyoming.

His exploits began immediately upon his return to Antelope. In a tent near Pike's shack lived a bachelor named Will Reid. One evening Reid left his meal simmering on the stove while he went to the store for some potatoes. When he returned, he could only stare in surprise. A hole in the top of the canvas showed where the stove *had* been, and the stewpans in which he had left his meal cooking were piled on the table, still warm. But the stove was certainly gone!

At a loss to guess who could have pulled such a trick, Reid went outside and looked around. Quickly he observed a new pipe through the roof of the shack occupied by Pike, with smoke rising from it.

He approached the place grimly, and the genial Pike met him at the door.

"Good evening, Will," he said heartily. "How's everything?"

Reid didn't answer. He shoved past him into the shack, and at one side he saw his stove—with a fire blazing in it and supper bubbling in Pike's stewpans.

"That's my stove!" stormed Reid. "And I'm going to take it!"

"Why, Will," Pike replied sorrowfully, "you shouldn't be saying that. Sounds like you think I'm not honest. Just stop and think. Your stove had four legs, didn't it? Well, this one has only three. Your stove had four lids on top, too, and this one has only three."

That was true. Reid felt suddenly deflated. But not so much that he couldn't see that one of the legs of the stove had been removed and that three bricks had taken its place. One of the lids also had been replaced by a piece of tin.

The outlandish piece of petty thievery rocked the countryside. Reid made every possible attempt to prove ownership to the stove, with the result, according to records, that he was left in a "ridiculous light" and Pike in "gleeful possession."

In September, 1885, the railroad reached the settlements up the Platte. The townsite company had laid out the town of Douglas half a mile south of Antelope, and the tent city was quickly absorbed by the new influx when the population jumped to twenty-five hundred in sixty days.

A cattleman named Curt Sears offered George Pike a partnership in a small ranch on Duck Creek, forty miles north, and Pike left Douglas. And began a record for horse stealing that had never before, and never since, been equaled!

For the next fifteen years there were few terms of court when George Pike did not appear on the docket on at least two counts. He hired Fred Harvey, one of Wyoming's most brilliant lawyers, paying him an annual salary, and Pike, the horse-stealing specialist, was never convicted of a crime and never served a term in the penitentiary.

Usually his defense was an alibi. In one case, when the evidence was heavily against him, a Mexican took the stand and testified that the morning of the alleged theft Pike had eaten breakfast with him on Pine Ridge, many miles away.

Later, when a friend asked Pike if he *had* eaten breakfast with the Mexican, Pike grinned.

"Sure did," he said, "but it was a year ago. I got the fellow to believing he had his dates mixed, that's all. He was so sure he was telling the truth he convinced everybody else."

Everybody loved George Pike, even those from whom he stole. Some even claimed he was generous—a kind of Robin Hood horse thief. Once he stole a horse from a poor man named Niedeauer who, when he could get no satisfaction from the authorities, took the bull by the horns and went straight to Pike. When Niedeauer explained that he didn't have enough money to buy another horse, the genial Pike said, waving a hand grandly toward his well-stocked corral:

"Oh, that's all right. Go down there and pick out one for yourself. Tell the boys I sent you."

One day Bob Carey, who owned the CY ranch, looked Pike up in a saloon.

"Pike," he said, "you've been stealing CY stock, and we know it! From now on my men will be on the lookout for you, and if you show your face inside CY fences again, they'll shoot to kill! I've come to give you a piece of advice, George. Be a good fellow, and keep away from there."

Pike grinned. "All right, Bob," he agreed. "I'll tell you what I'll do. You give me a twenty-dollar bill, and we'll call it square."

His audacity was unbelievable, even for the old West.

When he was charged with the theft of an expensive saddle from a man named John Morton, Pike swore someone put it on his horse to get even with him. He was acquitted.

Nor did George Pike stick strictly to the horse stealing on which his reputation was based. There are stories about how he "rolled" drunks, intimidated greenhorns, and once held up the saloon run by George Smith, and ran out the door, tossing the loot on top of the awning to be recovered later, and other tales too numerous to relate in brief.

But the tables finally were turned on George Pike. He had been so successful for years that he got to feeling that he had grown too big for any ordinary man to try to tilt against him. So he decided there was no longer any need for paying a lawyer, and he fired Fred Harvey.

That was the beginning of the end. Two months later he rode into Douglas, boiling mad. Will Reid, the man who had lost his stove in Antelope years before, had stolen a horse from Pike's pasture, the specialist in such thievery accused. It was something he wouldn't stand for, and had no intention of doing!

The story was too amazing to be true! But it was. And a tide of laughter swept down the valley.

Pike didn't think it was funny at all. He swore out a warrant for Reid. Reid was arrested and bound over for trial in the next term of court. Pike was so confident Reid would be convicted that he promised to buy drinks for the whole town and range if Reid should be freed.

Reid asked a lawyer, Charles F. Maurer, to defend him.

He showed Maurer a bill of sale for the horse and claimed he had purchased the animal from a Mormon emigrant who had passed through the country a few days before. Maurer knew well enough the paper was a forgery, and he wanted no part of it. Still his sympathies were with the man whom Pike had victimized so long ago—and got away with it. So he told Reid that his only hope was to get Fred Harvey, who was onto all George Pike's tricks.

"Pay him two hundred and fifty dollars," Maurer said, "and ask him to plead for you before the jury. You won't go wrong."

Reid did hire Harvey. And on the day of the trial everybody for miles around flocked to Douglas.

Pike's evidence was presented, and it was conclusive. One witness swore he had tracked Reid from the pasture. Another testified he had seen Reid leading the horse away. Pike smiled triumphantly.

Then Fred Harvey, the lawyer he had discharged, rose to his feet and addressed the jury.

"Gentlemen," he said, "I find myself in a rather interesting position today." He emphasized the fact that he had come there to defend Will Reid for stealing a horse from George Pike, then added, "Now, gentlemen, Pike is a horse thief himself. I know, because I defended him for fifteen years." He paused, and there was a ripple of merriment before he went on. "Once he told me that if he ever had a horse in his pasture that he had come by honestly, he would shoot it so it would not contaminate the rest."

The proceedings were suspended while the court and the jury recovered from convulsions.

The lawyer talked on for fifteen minutes, interrupted frequently by fresh outbursts of laughter. Not from George

Pike. Finally Harvey made his closing remark:

"Now, gentlemen, how in the name of justice can you conscientiously convict the defendant, Will Reid, of stealing a horse from George Pike, when you know perfectly well that Pike himself stole the horse in the first place?"

With the whole courtroom in an uproar, the jurymen rose to their feet and without leaving the box brought in a verdict of "Not Guilty."

George Pike was busy for a whole week passing out and paying for drinks. After that he sent word to all law officers up and down the Platte Valley that he was through.

"Look for somebody else from now on," he told them.

And there is no evidence that he ever stole anything else the rest of his life.

When he died in 1908, he was buried in a little cemetery on the hill east of Douglas, and his friends passed the hat to erect a stone over his grave. On it appears this epitaph:

> Underneath this stone in eternal rest
> Sleeps the wildest one of the wayward West;
> He was a gambler, sport, and cowboy, too,
> And he led the pace in an outlaw crew.
> He was sure on the trigger, and stayed to the end,
> But he was never known to quit a friend.
> In the relation of death all mankind is alike,
> But in life there was only one George W. Pike.

3. Thomas J. Smith

Tamer of Abilene

KANSAS was born in bitterness and weaned on gun-smoke. Before the Civil War it was a trophy for the bitterly competing slave and free states. And after the conflict there began a hardly less violent chapter in its history.

The renewed movement of settlers to the West brought steel rails to Abilene. The city became the closest market for Texas cattle and mushroomed into a brawling paradise where gun-toting cowboys—starved for whisky and women—made up for hardships on the trail in saloons, dance halls, and brothels. It was also a mecca for gamblers, thieves, and swindlers.

In its man-for-breakfast heyday, murderers flourished and boasted boisterously of its sinful reputation: "Too wild to be curried—too tough to be tamed!" Certainly, when Thomas J. Smith arrived there in 1870, it was a spawning place for Satan's best prospects.

A town council, organized in 1869 with T. C. Henry as mayor, had adopted ordinances to secure some semblance of decency. Thirty-two saloons were licensed, closing hours established, and dives forced back from the business center to Texas Street.

The carrying of firearms in town limits was prohibited. This order was posted conspicuously on bulletin boards erected at main roadways leading into the city.

To put teeth in their laws, town fathers provided for construction of a jail and the appointment of a marshal. That Abilene was to be reduced to a peaceful footing swept the plains from the Gulf to the Rockies, and Thomas J. Smith was among the first applicants for the job of marshal.

Inspecting candidate Smith, Mayor Henry saw a stalwart, broad-shouldered fellow about thirty, six feet tall, one hundred seventy pounds. He had been born in New York City, he said, of Irish parents. Henry noted his Celtic origin in his fair complexion, auburn hair and mustache, and bluish-gray eyes.

Smith mentioned no living relatives or what had brought him West. There were shadowy details of wanderings in Utah and Nevada, and employment in various capacities along the Nebraska frontier on Union Pacific Railroad construction.

While working in Bear River, Wyoming, in 1868, he had won the nickname of "Bear River Tom" by playing a prominent part in a gun battle there. After that, he had served as peace officer of several terminus towns. At the time, he was marshal of Kit Carson, Colorado.

Mayor Henry was impressed with his gentle manner. His low, evenly modulated voice and simple, direct speech inspired confidence. But the mayor thought he was too soft spoken to control the violent Texans and rejected him. Bear River Tom thanked him, left his address, and returned to Kit Carson.

After he had gone, details of the Bear River riot drifted to Henry. Businessmen had organized a town government to put down lawlessness, but had been unsuccessful until Tom Smith, a revolver blazing in each hand, drove a group of armed invaders into a log storeroom. There they barricaded themselves until Smith—his fury spent and badly wounded —coolly marched away to the house of a friend to await the arrival of troops from Fort Bridger.

He was no two-gun man with notches on his pistols. He shot only if necessary.

"Anyone can bring in a dead man," Smith said. "A good officer is one who brings them in alive."

Both Bear River, Wyoming, and Kit Carson, Colorado, had been end-of-the-track towns where cowboys, soldiers, buffalo hunters, teamsters, and railroad men gathered to raise havoc until Tom Smith took over. When they got too boisterous, Smith strode among them. If they didn't do as he said, he knocked them down and disarmed them or locked them in jail.

But Abilene was different, thought Mayor Henry. The town had developed civilizing influences. There was a stone schoolhouse, two churches, and a newspaper. The county was building a two-story brick courthouse, and in the center of Texas Street, across from the Bull's Head Saloon, other workers were finishing the walls of a small stone jail.

Ironically, Henry's conception of Smith changed once he heard the Bear River story. Now he thought Smith was too notorious, and he appointed a local man.

Cattle season had just opened. Invading Texans dunked

Mayor T. C. Henry who hired Tom Smith to be marshal of Abilene. *Courtesy Kansas State Historical Society.*

"Bear River" Tom Smith who enforced Abilene town council's order forbidding carrying of six-shooters or other weapons.

the new marshal. Firearms warnings at entrances to the city were shot full of holes and torn down. Another group of exuberant Lone Star natives, considering the stone jail an insult, demolished its walls.

Henry hired another marshal, had the jail rebuilt under day and night guard. Then a cook from a trail outfit shot out the street lamps and got locked up.

With a rebel yell, angry Texans swept down from the stockyards. They shot off the lock, and the cook fled to safety. Then they swirled back up the street, ordering all business houses to close, invading some of them on horseback and shooting up the places, and burying a parting fusillade in the mayor's building.

Other marshals tried after that, failed, and resigned. In desperation, the mayor appealed to the St. Louis police. The chief of police obliged by sending two men.

The Texans heard they were coming. When the policemen got off the train and started downtown, they found themselves amid the greatest carnival of lawless deviltry Abilene had yet witnessed. They fled back to the station, glad to escape with their lives, and took the return train.

Now the cowboys really took over. They galloped up and down the roadway to the stockyards, shooting in the air, challenging anyone to stop them. Mayor Henry was ridiculed and abused, the blinds on his office windows were ripped down and broken, and his associates insulted.

Town trustees wanted to be firm, yet they didn't want to kill the goose that laid the golden egg. The Chisholm Trail had become significant to the development of the country. But Texas Street had to be civilized. Any moment these Texans might ride forth, a destroying horde wiping out farm-

Cowboys whooping it up in Abilene dance hall. *From Joseph McCoy's* Historic Sketches of the Cattle Trade, *1874*.

McCoy's Abilene, first and perhaps wildest of cattle-trail towns. *From Joseph McCoy's* Historic Sketches of the Cattle Trade, *1874.*

ing interests, seizing what could be used for their cattle, taking over Abilene.

Days and nights dragged in sleepless suspense with predictions mounting as to what violence would occur next.

Both the home-brand and imported eastern talent had failed. Despite his reputation, Bear River Tom Smith had so much the manner of a reserved, self-respecting citizen that Mayor Henry still considered him too quiet to whip the cowboys into line. But, as a last resort, he sent for him.

When he arrived, Henry looked him over again and felt even worse than before. Smith wasn't even wearing a gun!

"It's plenty rough," the mayor warned. "Things have got out of hand. Why don't you look around today, then come back? You might not want the job."

Bear River Tom grinned. "I looked around when I rode in on Silverheels. But I'll do as you say."

Smith rode up Texas Street past the Lone Star Saloon, the Bull's Head, the Alamo, and the Old Fruit, but he didn't stop. He drifted out of town and spent the day seeing the stockyards and the creek bridge, returning to the mayor's office about sundown.

"I haven't seen anything different," he reported.

Henry felt uneasy. Trying to pierce Smith's nonchalance, he asked: "You think you can put an end to this lawlessness?"

Smith nodded.

"How?" the mayor demanded.

"Pistols and whisky don't mix. The pistols will have to go. Might as well contend with a maniac as an armed and drunken cowboy."

The mayor stared incredulously. "But these cowboys are wild. You saw what they have done to our gun ordinance."

"We'll post it up again," he said.

"They are a thousand to one. *How are you going to take away their guns?*"

"One at a time," Smith replied.

"Take a gun from a cowboy who sooner would kill you than not?"

"I think I can," Bear River Tom said quietly.

"It won't be no picnic," he added. "But that is the way it will have to be handled."

The mayor was frightened. Was he placing himself in a deluded man's hands? He nervously raked his mustache with a ruler. Then he thought again of the Bear River fight and stiffened.

"All right. I'll have new copies of the ordinance printed tonight. Our citizens are tired of being run over. They've bought town lots and built homes. The farmers have taken up government land and improved it. The Texans have bought nothing, paid nothing, own nothing. If they try to run us out, we'll get government troops from Riley and Harker—"

"I don't think it will be necessary," Smith interrupted. "Just swear me in."

After administering the oath, Mayor Henry said, "The town is now in your hands. That's all."

Smith clamped the big star on his shirt and gave the mayor's hand a firm grip. Then he mounted his big gray horse. "I'll pick up the new notices tonight and post them in the morning," he said.

As the mayor watched him depart, he noticed that Smith wore a revolver under his coat. "He's got nerve!" Henry said.

However, as he returned the Bible to his office, got his hat, and started home, Henry didn't expect to see Smith alive the next day.

Word of Smith's appointment had already sped ahead of him. Down the street a dozen men waited to try him. Big Hank, a huge Texan who had bullied his outfit up the trail and been particularly obnoxious to former marshals, shoved his belted revolver to the fore of his leg and swaggered up as Smith dismounted.

"You the guy who thinks he's going to run this town?" he asked.

Smith quietly admitted his identity. "There's an ordinance against carrying pistols," he added. "I'll trouble you for yours."

Big Hank broke into a coarse fit of profanity which meant, simply, that no man alive could take away his gun. Again Smith demanded the pistol, moving in close, holding out his hand for the weapon.

"Go to hell!" roared the trail hand. He backed away in a gun fighter's crouch, waiting for the marshal to draw.

Bear River Tom's outstretched hand moved, not for a gun, but swiftly upward in a balled fist against the cowboy's jaw. Big Hank sprawled backward into the dust and lay still. When he came to, he had been stripped of his artillery. Bear River Tom stood over him.

"Now hit for camp, or I'll lock you up." Astonished, the cowboy beat it—fast.

The news swept the cow camps. To the Texans, accustomed to drawing a gun and shooting it out, subduing a ruffian primed to kill simply by knocking him cold seemed strangely unorthodox.

In a camp on Chapman Creek, northwest of Abilene, a burly brute named Wyoming Frank swore the marshal had been lucky. Sheer surprise had caught Big Hank off guard. It couldn't happen again. Frank wagered that he could put a quick end to the new marshal's reign. Next morning he rode into town.

Smith was late appearing on the streets. A crowd gathered for the showdown. Impatient and a little tipsy, Wyoming Frank began boasting that the marshal probably had seen him ride in and "lit out."

Finally, Tom Smith appeared, walking slowly down the center of the roadway. Wyoming Frank straddled toward him, the butt of his big six-shooter pronged out from his thigh and his right hand hovering to draw at the drop of a hat.

"I hear you're collectin' shootin' irons, fellow," he called insolently.

The marshal walked up to him before replying. "That's right," he said, empty hand extended. "You'll have to give me yours. You're violating the law."

Frank refused, with a vile epithet. Smith stepped forward. Too late the cowboy found himself balked by the marshal's close reach.

He eased back, maneuvering for space to draw, but Smith followed. He backed off again, and Smith kept coming every step. Before he realized it, he had backed across the board-walk into a saloon.

He backed to the center of the room and stopped. Again Smith asked for his gun, and Frank cursed. Any second now he would make a desperate grab for his weapon and kill the marshal.

But again Smith's chain-lightning right shot out. Wyoming Frank staggered backward, and Smith pounced on him like a gamecock. A left and another right crumpled Frank on the floor.

"I'll give you five minutes to get out of town," Smith said, "and don't let me set eyes on you again."

The crowd was electrified. Suddenly, the saloon proprietor stepped behind the bar and handed Smith his revolver. "That was the nerviest act I ever seen," he said. "Here's my gun. I won't need it, I reckon, as long as you're marshal."

It was a signal to disarm, and the others came forward, offering their weapons.

"Leave them with the bartender until you are ready to go back to camp," Smith said.

From that moment Tom Smith was boss on both sides of the railroad. His cool courage won the instant support of even the toughest Texan. They realized that he didn't want to kill them as the other marshals had. They could have a good time and make all the noise they wanted to if they damaged no property.

He persuaded hotelkeepers to store pistols of the drovers and other guests and put up signs reading: ALL FIREARMS TO BE DEPOSITED WITH THE PROPRIETOR. Guests garnished with revolvers doubtlessly frightened away many good people. It would mean more hotel business, money flowing in.

He took the saloonkeepers and store owners into the program. It meant more goods to sell, more customers. Abilene could be a place where they could bring their families, from whom most of them had been forced to live apart because of lawless conditions.

This maneuver placed the visitor on the defensive. The firearms ordinance informed him what he had to do upon entering the city. It cost him nothing to deposit his guns with friends. It was for him to act. He could not say he had not been warned.

Smith also invaded the houses of ill fame. Women needed no pistols with the men disarmed.

Gamblers and toughs became convinced that it was wise to obey Smith's order. His mettle had been tested; the performance had left no room for doubt.

It became the fashion not to wear guns on the streets of Abilene. Although drunkenness, quarreling, and dens of iniquity flourished, there was no promiscuous shooting in town limits the rest of 1870.

Town trustees confirmed Smith's appointment without hesitation. They set his salary at $150 for the first month, but as arrests became more frequent, they raised it to $225, and set up a police court for quick trials. Cantankerous men left town at the point of the marshal's pistol.

All summer Smith's gray horse Silverheels was a familiar figure on Abilene streets. Bear River Tom had originated the idea of checking the cowboys' guns and was the first frontier marshal to patrol a town on horseback.

Smith knew the fighting advantage of a mounted man over an adversary on foot. Shooting a mounted man was more difficult. The movements of the animal complicated matters. Besides, Texans loved horses too much to take chances of getting an animal hurt or killed.

Smith rode his gray in the middle of the street. It was easy to kill an officer from a window or doorway if he stayed on the sidewalk. But from the seat of a horse the marshal could spot anyone waiting ahead of him, or on either side.

Despite all this taming, policing Abilene was a hard job. The population of Texas Street was constantly shifting. New herds of beef brought new bands of cowboys. Every train from the East brought new gamblers and toughs. They knew nothing in advance of the ordinances or the marshal's efforts to preserve order.

Smith was forced to deal with them as he had with Big Hank. Though he was shot at occasionally, he never seemed to get hit, and continued to rely on his strength and agility to keep the peace.

Only once did he have to use the big revolver at his hip. This happened in the Old Fruit Saloon.

A Texan had deliberately kept his pistol in violation of the ordinance. Tom found him drinking with a dozen of his tough cronies.

It was the cheapest saloon in Abilene—a long, narrow room with chairs and tables on one side and a bar on the other that ran half the length of the wall. Most buildings in Abilene had back doors opening into alleys, but the Old Fruit had only a side entrance.

The offender and his cronies were talking and didn't see Smith enter. They sighted him as he approached and instinctively split into two groups, forming a row on each side of the narrow enclosure. The cowboy with the pistol retreated to the rear of the room.

Six-shooter drawn, his eyes sweeping the two rows of antagonists, Smith moved steadily toward his quarry. As he passed down the lane, the punchers closed in behind him. Smith read the psychology of the bunch. They had been drinking too much; they were without a leader; they jostled one another, waiting to see who would get up the gumption to shoot first.

He had almost reached the cowboy when a melee broke out behind him. Two of the drunks grabbed pistols from behind the bar and began firing. But only other Texans received bullet wounds.

Smith was protected by the group. They could not fire at him without hitting their friends. The uproar intensified. Knives were drawn, but no one wanted to get within range of the marshal's fists!

Suddenly, one drunk thought of the lamps. He snatched one from its bracket and hurled it at the marshal. It struck the floor at Tom's feet. The glass failed to break, but the flame flickered ominously.

If it exploded, the place and everybody in it would burn.

A hush swept the crowd. They recalled such a holocaust only a few weeks before when exploding kerosene had killed the wife of a railroad section boss and destroyed four buildings.

But luckily the lamp didn't explode, and by this time Smith had reached his man. Covered by the marshal's pistol, he offered no resistance. Smith collared him, disarmed him, and tossed him over his shoulder. As he stalked through the darkness toward the dim glow of the door and crossed the street to the jail, the cowboys let him go.

If they fired a shot, they might kill their pard, sprawled across his back.

The audacity of the deed palsied Texas Street. What manner of man this who could not be scared or shot or burned? The superstitious thought he bore a charmed life. The Texans swore he wore a steel plate under his shirt.

There was metal about him—iron will.

He kept silent about his past, and the mystery about him grew. Mayor Henry believed, years later, that had he taken time to probe into Smith's personal history, it would have been one of the frontier wonder tales.

Smith neither drank nor gambled, something unique among early peace officers. The mayor never heard him curse or tell a questionable story. Yet he held no puritanical views of other people's conduct. The town had laid down the rules. He only asked that people obey them.

He smiled often, made friends easily, and was very fond of children. In their conversations together, Henry could tell he had been well educated.

Where had a man of such breeding learned to handle Texans? He was neither Texan, Yankee, nor Civil War veteran.

Only once did Smith drop one other morsel of his past. He told Henry that for a time, before coming West, he had served on the New York City police department. It was there that he had learned to ride, box, and shoot straight.

People by and large rejoiced that law had come to Abilene, and they expressed their deepest gratitude by presenting their marshal with a brace of pearl-handled revolvers.

The cattle country witnessed a great influx of excellent families who built farms, bought town lots, and built more homes and stores. The town prospered.

Out on the plains Texas cattlemen suffered more difficulty. Their herds raided gardens and spring crops and farmers demanded settlement. Disgruntled at these attempts to ruin the plains for the cattle industry, the Texans were not friendly. Sometimes they bluffed the granger, but more often they begrudgingly paid the damage.

They were in a bad mood when they reached Abilene but here, too, they soon learned to be satisfied with the way Tom Smith ran things.

It was ironic that Smith should come to his death, not at the hands of Texans, but by persons he had protected from them.

On October 23, 1870, Andrew McConnell, a Scot with an

ugly disposition, shot and killed John Shea, who had driven some cattle across his land on Chapman Creek and destroyed his corn. A warrant was sworn out for murder, and Sheriff Joseph Cramer rode out to arrest McConnell.

McConnell took refuge in a dugout on his farm, armed himself, and informed the sheriff he would not be taken alive. Cramer came back to Abilene for help. Tom Smith volunteered to bring him in. Accompanied by Deputy James McDonald, he rode to the dugout. It was built into a hillside and the door opened into the end of a ditch.

As they approached, McConnell and a friend, Moses Miles, who lived on a neighboring farm, were down the slope chopping wood. Spying the officers, the men dropped their implements and made for the dugout.

The officers reached the spot, cutting off Miles, but McConnell got into the dugout and locked the door. Leaving McDonald to guard Miles, Smith leaped from his horse and descended the dirt steps.

"This is Marshal Smith, McConnell!" he shouted through the door. "Open up and come out."

There was no answer.

Smith threw his broad shoulders against the door. It creaked and splintered open. The marshal plunged inside. McConnell, facing him across the room, raised his rifle and fired. The muzzle exploded in Smith's face; the ball tore into his chest.

Recoiling, Smith fired one shot in return. The bullet tore into McConnell's right hand, forcing him to drop his weapon. Then, though seriously wounded, Smith grappled him.

Outside, McDonald was trying to keep Miles from going into the dugout. He couldn't tell whether the farmer was armed, but kept warning him to stay back. Miles refused, and McDonald was so afraid he might produce a gun and start shooting that he made no effort to search him.

When the shots were fired inside and he saw Smith stagger back into the doorway, he was certain McConnell had killed the marshal. Fear seized the deputy. McConnell might appear in the doorway, shooting at him.

With no warning cry he fled across the prairie, leaving his horse where it was tied. At the nearest claim he found another pony, mounted, and rode to Abilene, announcing that Tom Smith had been slain.

Meanwhile, Smith had dragged McConnell outside the dugout, thinking McDonald was still holding off Miles. He wrestled McConnell to the ground, and had taken out the irons for his wrists when Miles came up behind him with an ax. He struck Smith in the neck three times.

When McDonald returned with a posse, they found Tom Smith dead, his head almost completely severed from his body.

Miles and McConnell had fled, but they were captured a few days later. Enraged citizens wanted to hang them, including the deputy who had ridden with Smith and then skipped out on him. But long prison terms met the demands of an outraged people.

Tom Smith's body, lying on a bed of straw in a wagon, was brought in. The entire country turned out for the most elaborate funeral Abilene could afford. Crepe fluttered from hats, arms, and bosoms as the procession wound through Texas Street.

Behind the hearse, banked with branches and flowers, walked Smith's big gray horse Silverheels. From the pommel of the saddle hung Bear River Tom's brace of pearl-handled revolvers.

Over his grave Abilene citizens erected a granite monument. The inscription reads:

THOMAS J. SMITH
MARSHAL OF ABILENE, 1870
DIED A MARTYR TO DUTY, NOV. 2, 1870
A FEARLESS HERO OF FRONTIER DAYS,
WHO IN COWBOY CHAOS,
ESTABLISHED THE SUPREMACY OF LAW.

4. Wal Henderson

Hellion of Humbug Gulch

HE was a rough giant of a man, Wal Henderson, with the courage of a she-grizzly, and a dead shot with revolver or rifle. A Missourian by birth, he had come over the mountains to New Mexico in 1871, soon after the discovery of gold in the Moreno hills. He staked a claim in Humbug Gulch, and apparently had settled down to a quiet, honest life—then, virtually overnight, he became a terror to the whole mountain population, a desperado of the first order.

It happened like this . . .

One afternoon Wal decided to do a little prospecting in another part of the range. His claim in the Gulch was only partially opened, and to prevent someone jumping it in his absence, he got one of his more educated neighbors to come over and cut his name on a dead pine stump near the mouth of the pit.

With a keen bowie the neighbor slashed out a huge "WAL henderSoN his Klaime." It took him nearly two hours to complete his literary labors, while Wal stood by and watched, a grin spreading wider and wider across his moon face.

"Well," Wal decided finally, "ain't nobody goin' to touch that now."

He swung his pick and shovel over his shoulder, took his bearing from the sun, and trotted off down the canyon.

He was gone three days. When he returned, he found his claim jumped by a party of Irish miners who had just arrived in the diggings. As quietly as his bulldog nature would permit, Wal told them to "Git!" But they swore they would hold the claim and fight him "even if he was as big as Finn MaCool."

Wal held his temper. Coolly he strode to his cabin. He armed himself with a revolver, a Spencer carbine, a wicked IXL blade, and returned to the gulch.

"Git out o' there—quick! Jump!" he yelled. "Or I'll fill you full o' lead!"

The angry trio swarmed out of the hole. Their leader lurched toward Wal, swinging his miner's shovel to lay him out with a single blow. Wal raised his pistol and fired, and the Irishman fell dead with a bullet between his eyes.

His two frightened companions fled, and Wal returned to his cabin to rest up from his trip, the incident forgotten.

The two miners went into camp, told a story of brutal attack and murder, and a mob swarmed up to Wal's place and carried him away to the little log jail.

As the news spread, Irish miners flocked in from the hills, openly proclaiming they intended to take Wal out at dark and hang him and that they would fight any element who resisted them.

The jail was an abandoned log store with a dirt-and-brush roof, a stone fireplace in one corner, and a large chimney yawning against the sky. Shortly after dark a motley, drunken crowd appeared at the jail. They ran the guard away with pistol shots and broke open the door.

The room was empty. A quick examination by a few sober members of the group showed that Wal had escaped up the chimney, concealed himself on the roof, and during the excitement below, leaped to the ground and fled into the hills.

The rest of the night and all next day they scoured every building and hole where he might possibly be hiding. But they didn't find him.

Wal had fortified himself in an abandoned tunnel a hundred yards up the gulch. Being so close to town, no one had thought to look for him there.

About midnight, after the search had died down, he slipped into camp, broke into a stable, and saddled a horse, and rode to Taos. He sent the horse back to its owner, complimenting him on the endurance of the animal and for building a structure that could be entered so easily.

Two weeks later Wal rode down the street of the startled camp on a Mexican pony with a pair of revolvers buckled around his waist and a carbine slung across his shoulders. Halting in front of Joe Stinson's saloon, he swung down with a devil-may-care nod to the loafers on the sidewalk, and invited them in for a drink.

Leaning at the bar, he related his adventures since he had been away. He had returned to look after his mining interests, he said, and anyone with ideas to the contrary was welcome to test the battery of weapons he had brought along. Receiving no objections, Wal tossed off another glass of "Taos lightning," as whisky was called, quietly mounted his horse, and rode out to his cabin.

Back in camp, the excitement died down. It was finally agreed that if Wal kept away from Humbug Gulch, they would leave him alone.

For a month Wal settled down to working his claim. One morning he came to town for supplies. He was sitting in Stinson's saloon when a party of half-drunk Irish miners entered.

A remark was passed about Wal's claim and their murdered companion. One of the miners approached Wal with a knife in his hand.

"Bejabbers," he said, "you'd look better cut to pieces than hanged."

A pistol flashed in Wal's hand, leveled at the Irishman's head. "Drop that knife!" Wal said.

The knife clattered on the floor. Wal replaced his weapon and finished his drink.

The gang was bent for trouble, but Wal was not to be intimidated. He relaxed with his back to the wall, lighted his pipe, and began smoking.

He listened to their coarse jests and threats for nearly half an hour. Finally his patience wore thin. When one of them made a filthy reference, Wal leaped to his feet.

"By Judas, I think I'll kill you just for luck and stop this damn foolishness!"

He whipped out his pistol and fired. The victim fell dead with a ball in the center of his forehead.

The shot brought a crowd rushing inside. But no one attempted to arrest Wal. He waited against the side of the room until the sheriff and alcalde arrived, then surrendered.

They took him to his old quarters—the little log jail. The drunken companions of the dead miner immediately began mustering another crowd to hang Wal.

This time every precaution was taken to prevent his escape. An extra guard was posted on the outside, and two men watched the roof.

When Wal heard the mob howling in the distance, he stepped close to the side of the door. As it crashed from its hinges, and the crowd plunged into the dark room, Wal quietly stepped past them into the street, circled the building, and vanished in the night.

The miners were enraged that Wal had outwitted them again. They trailed him to his cabin. But Wal had already been there, got his horse, and by this time was far into the hills.

The mob returned to Humbug Gulch, swearing to kill him on sight. But when Wal dropped into town a couple of days later, no one molested him.

He rode in and out of camp every few days after that, and everyone moved about quietly. The matter seemed to have ended by mutual agreement.

One morning the camp buzzed with a report of the robbery of the mail stage in the canyon between Ute Creek and Elizabethtown. The coach made triweekly trips between Humbug Gulch and the Cimarron River to connect with the southern line of the Overland. At a lonely spot where the canyon narrowed and the road wound around a hillside covered with scrubby pine, a masked bandit had pointed a rifle at the driver, ordered him to throw the express box off the boot, then drive on.

Within a month six such holdups occurred. The law-abiding populace became aroused. Posses scoured the canyon, but found no trace of the robber or his hideout. They were convinced that he was someone in their midst, who knew when favorable conditions existed.

They noted that Wal was gone from camp a day or two each time a holdup occurred. Wal would always show up the morning after and "demurely ride through town" as if nothing had happened. It was "murmured about" that he could shed a lot of light on the depredations if he would talk.

In fact, Wal never mentioned the subject, nor expressed an opinion when it was being discussed in his presence.

Joe Stinson, the proprietor of the saloon Wal so frequently patronized, and where many of these discussions took place, was a professional gambler. His knowledge of monte, faro, and poker made him as much a terror behind the green-covered table as a highwayman along the dark trails, and Stinson never hesitated to fleece an unsuspecting victim.

One evening, when a discussion of the robberies was at its height, Stinson remarked:

"The damned rascal can't live a great ways from this camp, and I would help hang the mother's son, by Judas, if we could catch him."

For the first time Wal appeared concerned. He stated that he had more respect for a stage robber than for some of the "pretty-talking thieves" in the boom towns who "stole through a damned old faro box."

Stinson flushed. Realizing there would be trouble if the conversation continued, he said:

"Come on, let's all have a drink and go home."

Wal stepped to the bar, and Stinson asked: "What will you have?"

"Whisky," Wal said.

Stinson shoved out a bottle and glass, and while he mixed himself a toddy behind the counter, Wal suddenly grabbed the bottle and emptied it on the bar.

"If you don't like what I said," he growled, "you know what

you can do about it!" And his hand dropped to his hip as if reaching for his gun.

Stinson seized a pistol from under the counter and fired. Wal dropped dead with a bullet in his brain.

Stinson gave himself up. When the alcalde arrived, the facts were related, and the jury brought in a verdict of justifiable homicide.

They buried Wal Henderson on a little hill above Humbug Gulch, where short months before he had staked his claim.

Beadle's Dime New York Library

COPYRIGHTED IN 1881, BY BEADLE & ADAMS.

ENTERED AT THE POST OFFICE AT NEW YORK, N. Y., AT SECOND CLASS MAIL RATES.

Vol. XIII. | Published Every Week. | *Beadle & Adams, Publishers,* 98 WILLIAM STREET, N. Y., December 21, 1881. | Ten Cents a Copy. $5.00 a Year. | No. 165

JOAQUIN, THE TERRIBLE.

The True History of the Three Bitter Blows that Changed an Honest Man to a Merciless Demon.

BY JOSEPH E. BADGER, JR.,

AUTHOR OF "EQUINOX TOM," "SOL SCOTT," "ALABAMA JOE," "JACK RABBIT," "CAPTAIN COOL-BLADE," "PACIFIC PETE," ETC., ETC.

JOAQUIN, THE TERRIBLE.

Caption on this cover of *Beadle's New York Dime Library* read: "Joe Stokes never won the dime novel fame of Joaquin Murieta (above), but he was classed in the ranks of those who spread death and terror the length and breadth of the West Coast, and was described by at least one San Francisco judge as 'the most dangerous man in California.'"

5. Joe Stokes

Forgotten Filibuster

WHEN Joe Stokes arrived in California from New York
in 1848, the whole territory from San Francisco to Los
Angeles, from the seashore to the base of the Sierra Nevada,
resounded with the cry of "Gold! Gold! Gold!"

News of its discovery at Sutter's Mill had spread like wild-
fire up and down the Pacific coast, traversed the continent
to the shores of the Atlantic, and within a few months
startled the whole civilized world.

Joe Stokes was just one of the many thousands caught up
in the tumultuous confluence of innumerable streams of emi-
gration pouring across the Rocky Mountains, around Cape
Horn, and from the barbarous and civilized countries across
the sea.

Miners already were at work in every large stream on the
western slope from the Feather to the Tuolomne River, and
in the northwestern corner of the Sacramento Valley. Law-

yers, clergymen, physicians, hotelkeepers, merchants, clerks, traders, farmers had left their occupations for the basket and spade. Homes stood empty, grass threatened village streets, and deserted ships swung at anchor in silent harbors. Even the garrison at Monterey abandoned arms for pickax and shovel.

Everyone was getting rich. But Joe Stokes, for some reason, drifted down to Sacramento and took a job keeping books in a dry-goods store.

He showed little interest in the fact that $3,000,000 worth of gold dust was exported from San Francisco in one week in 1850, that in August of that year monthly shipments reached $8,000,000; and hardly noticed the newspaper headlines on September 15, 1850, which reported 684 vessels in San Francisco harbor, waiting to exchange their produce for gold.

But he watched with interest the great rush to the mines from 1848 to 1850 exhaust the supply of beef cattle in the counties north of San Luis Obispo, and buyers flock to Los Angeles, the greatest cattle center in the state. Several good seasons of rain and grass had increased cattle and horses in the southern counties to an unprecedented number. Cattle brought twenty to thirty dollars per head, and many a first-class ranchero, who sold thousands at one time, considered his profits small change. The streets thronged with caballeros wearing suits costing as much as $500, riding splendid horses with saddles and trappings costing nearly $2,000.

In the coast cities and in the new towns that sprang up like magic in this glittering land of no law, no restraint, there was reckless speculation, excesses of all kinds, and disastrous conflagrations. Anarchy reared its ugly head.

A severe code was established. Thievery called for the startling penalty of a brand on the cheek with mutilation of the ears. Robbery and bloodshed were more severely punished. The difficulty lay in bringing about some semblance of law and order. For the scum of the four corners of the world had gathered here to prey on the land, gamble, drink, and fight.

Joe Stokes witnessed bloody raids, border warfare, and reprisals; he read of travelers waylaid and assassinated; he saw men's ears cut off, strung up, and paraded as trophies in barrooms, and heads severed from bleeding trunks kicked along public streets.

In 1852 the common query at the bar and breakfast table was, "How many were killed last night?" The only protection for human life and property was self-defense.

The Crescent City abounded with such places of vice as the Empire, Woodcock, and Humboldt, and Joe, "extremely gentlemanly in his manners, and almost timid in his retiring modesty," frequented the Woodcock and Humboldt to relax from a hard day at his books and "buck a slug or two."

There was a gambler at the Humboldt named Tom Collins, who ran a monte bank, and could handle a Colt or bowie knife with the best artists of the time. One night when Joe was bucking he caught Collins drawing waxed cards and accused him of cheating.

Collins frowned on Joe like a lion frowning on a rat, and gave him two minutes to leave the place.

"And if I don't?" Joe queried.

"Then I will kill you!" Collins sprang to his feet, whipped out his revolver, and fired a shot over Joe's head.

Joe didn't move. Quietly he folded his arms and told Collins, "I am unarmed. If you are cowardly enough to shoot me, blaze away. I won't run."

Collins fired two more shots. The first clipped a lock from

Joe's hair, the second burned between his arm and body. But Joe remained within ten feet of the gambler, defiantly looking him in the eye.

Collins fired again. The bullet tore into Joe's left arm. Blood soaked his sleeve. At that moment a bystander tossed Joe a loaded revolver.

Collins ducked behind a column supporting the ceiling and fired another shot at Joe, which missed him. Joe took deliberate aim at the gambler's head, the only portion of his body sticking from behind the column. The bullet struck Collins in the neck, killing him instantly.

The slaying placed Joe Stokes in the arena of the desperado, and for the next three years he became classed in the ranks of Crooked Nose Smith, Cherokee Bob, Rattlesnake Dick, Jesus Tejada, Sheet-Iron Jack, and Joaquin Murieta, who spread death and terror the length and breadth of the West coast.

Little is known of Joe's early life. Major Horace Bell, the California Ranger, detailing Joe's adventures in his reminiscences many years later, claimed he was the brother of E. S. Stokes, who shot and killed Jim Fisk, the great American stock manipulator who made a fortune out of government contracts and by smuggling cotton through the lines during the Civil War. His father was a banker in Philadelphia.

Perhaps this accounted for Joe's temperament. Unlike the other bad men of the day, Joe never picked a quarrel, and was always in good humor. But he was calculating and cool. As one judge put it, after fining him for an affray in San Francisco in 1855, he was "without a doubt the most dangerous man in California."

One of the toughest, noisiest little settlements on the coast was the old mission village of San Gabriel, nine miles from

Major Horace Bell, the California Ranger who said Joe Stokes was the most magnanimous bad man he ever knew.

Los Angeles. There were three saloons at the Mission, all operated by Americans, and doing a thriving business from early morning until late at night.

One set at the southwest corner of the old Mission building with a sign in large black letters across its whitewashed front proclaiming it "Headquarters." Why it was given this name no one knew, except that it was the largest and most pretentious of the three and the collecting point for free-spending army officers, vagabonds, and drunken, howling Indians whose favorite pastime was "splitting and quartering heads."

On fiesta days and Sunday, business was exceptionally good. Horse races and cockfights were put on for the public. Large crowds of bad men mingled with respectable citizens at the bar. Fights were frequent, and blood and whisky flowed freely.

General Josh Bean was proprietor until 1852. He was joined in April that year by his brother, Roy Bean, who had fled to California from Chihuahua, Mexico, after killing a Mexican. Roy later became famous in Texas as "The Law West of the Pecos."

About eleven o'clock one Sunday night in November General Bean was shot from his horse as he started home. Cipriano Sandoval, a gambler, was held for the murder; revenge because Bean had paid court to an Indian girl who had also captured Sandoval's affections was believed to be the motive. In his confession, Sandoval named Felipe Read, the right-hand man of Joaquin Murieta, as the slayer. Some said the Indian woman was Felipe's mistress and that Bean had seduced her. The wise ones claimed she was Murieta's own *querida,* and that the whole thing had been planned by the great Joaquin.

In any case, Cipriano and Read went to the gallows, and

posses were organized to bring in Murieta. Roy Bean rode
on at least one of these expeditions that finally resulted in
death for the notorious outlaw.

After General Bean's murder, Roy took over as proprietor
at Headquarters. He dressed in elegant Mexican costume,
and strode about like a cock of the walk, with a pair of navy
Colts on his belt and a silver-hilted bowie sheathed in one
of his red-topped boots.

One Sunday evening in December, 1854, the place was
jammed with nearly three hundred Americans, Indians, and
Mexicans. Whisky, aguardiente and angelica for the "femi-
nine angels" and mixture of squaws flowed at the bar. Two
monte games were in progress. Out back a cockfight and
Mexican circus were going on, and a horse race was getting
ready to start. The big room was loud with coarse talk and
laughter and reeked with whisky fumes and cigar smoke.

Dressed in usual Mexican garb, with bowie knife and
navies, Roy Bean "strode in and around, offering to bet on
his favorite cock, making a cow for the horse race . . . and
assuming all the importance of brief authority by lording it
over that reckless throng."

Joe Stokes, stylishly dressed and pale-faced, stepped in at
the front door. His neat appearance and modesty in approaching the bar and ordering a "refreshment" turned all
eyes in that den of cutthroats toward him. As he leaned at
the bar, a ruffian, whom no one knew by name, swaggered
toward him.

Pausing in front of Joe, feet planted apart, he surveyed the
youth from head to foot with a derisive grin.

"Whar the hell you from?" he asked.

Joe said, "Los Angeles."

"Yuh warn't raised thar?" demanded the bully.

Roy Bean, saloon operator in California before becoming famous as "The Law West of the Pecos." *Courtesy* Frontier Fix, *Ed. Bartholomew, Houston, Texas.*

Bean's headquarters in Langtry, Texas.

"No," Stokes replied. "I was reared in New York. You know where New York is, of course?"

"I jest don't; I reckon it's up north somewhar. Ain't thet so?"

"No, sir," Joe responded.

"I reckon it is!" thundered the bully, his demeanor becoming more overbearing. "Don't tell me whar New York is! Know who yer talkin' ter? Yer talkin' ter the Wild Wolf of the Arkansaw."

Then he announced loudly that he was "the bloodiest man in the Cherokee Nation." He was a half-breed from the Indian Territory; he had belonged to the Ridge party and had killed more Ross men than any dozen men in the party. He had shot two Mexicans in New Mexico and a soldier at Fort Yuma en route to California. He had been in California three weeks, and hadn't killed anyone yet.

"But yuh open yer trap once more," he shouted, "and I'll give these Mexicans a chance ter have a funeral."

Joe said ironically, "Sir, don't let them bury me alive."

At this moment Roy Bean shouldered between them. "You must stop molesting this boy," he said. "He is patronizing my place, and I will protect him."

Joe thanked Roy politely, and added: "This gentleman won't hurt anybody."

The "bloodiest man" erupted like a volcano. "Get outa my way!" he roared at Bean. "I'm going to kill him!"

The crowd rushed to the four doors, leaving the pair alone in the room. Joe leaned on the bar, smiling. The ruffian's hand touched his revolver, but before he could draw, a small pistol leaped from under Joe's coat, its muzzle pointed at the pit of the half-breed's stomach.

In a voice as polite and gentle as before, Joe said: "Get up your hands, or I'll kill you!"

The ruffian obeyed.

"Unbuckle your belt and drop your gun on the floor," Joe ordered, and the ruffian complied.

"Now, get back in that corner." The ruffian moved to the point indicated by the flourish of Joe's pistol. Then Joe picked up his revolver, shoved it under his belt, and called for a cigar.

The crowd was cautiously moving back inside to view the proceedings. Someone furnished a stogie, and Joe lighted it.

For a moment he puffed vigorously, keeping an eye on his foe. When the cigar was going well, he stepped up to the ruffian, ordered him to place his hands behind him, then said:

"I am going to stick the burning end of this cigar in your nose. Let it stay there until it goes out. If you flinch or sniffle, or try to remove it, it will be you whom these Mexicans give a funeral."

He thrust the fiery end of the cigar into the ruffian's nose and stepped back to the counter.

Keeping his pistol aimed, Joe took a full minute to finish his drink, while the cigar sizzled in the man's nostril. Then he said to Bean:

"Here is his revolver. When I am gone, give it to him."

Turning to the crowd, he announced: "My name is Joe Stokes. I can whip any man who don't like me, and I like to lay for such soft snaps as the Wild Wolf of the Arkansas."

A whoop and catcalls in English, and "Vive el muchacho tan valiente" in Mexican, echoed from the crowd, and the "bloodiest man" was pelted with empty glasses and bottles as he fled from the saloon. Joe Stokes became the "Napoleon of San Gabriel's Headquarters," and late in the afternoon he rode back to Los Angeles with Bean's friend, Major Bell.

In his reminiscences Bell described Stokes as the "bravest and most magnanimous" bad man he ever knew. Like the others, he became the victim of unsettled conditions in the Territory.

Crimes against life and property increased. The outlaws grew so bold, defiant, and successful that they formed an association, with a regular headquarters, under the name of "hounds." They operated throughout the cities and countryside as thieves, burglars, incendiaries, and assassins. Their number increased by scores of felons who had found their way to California from the convict islands of Van Dieman's Land and New South Wales. Their victims ran into the hundreds, and so inefficient and corrupt were the courts and enforcement agencies that every man not actually in league with the criminals was on the defensive, carrying his weapons by day and sleeping with them at night.

Outraged beyond endurance, well-disposed citizens, determined to take the law into their own hands and to administer that law in the interests of justice and self-protection, bound themselves into a powerful, voluntary organization called the "Vigilance Committee." Within a few short months terrible and repeated examples of swift justice at the hands of this committee cleansed San Francisco of the horde that infested its precincts. In Los Angeles and Sacramento similar scenes of retribution were enacted, and the summary execution of noted felons carried out in the smaller cities, until the work of reformation appeared finished and the committee existed as scarcely more than a nominal organization.

In 1856 crime again became rampant, and the committee was provoked into resumption of its work by the murder of General Richardson, the United States marshal, by Charles Cora, unconvicted because the jury couldn't agree, and the

Hanging of a Mexican girl for murder of a miner at Somers-ville, California, in 1851. *From* Munsey's Magazine, *1901.*

Artist's sketch of the first execution carried out by the San Francisco Vigilance Committee of 1851. *From* Munsey's Magazine, *1901.*

deliberate and cold-blooded murder of James King, editor of the *Evening Bulletin,* by James P. Casey, editor of the *Sunday Times,* both of San Francisco. They stormed the jail, took Charles Cora, with Casey, and hanged them on scaffolds constructed in front of committee headquarters.

Extending its operations into Sacramento, Stockton, San Jose, and other places of crime, the committee executed at least four felons who had gone unpunished by the courts, drove many more from the state, and "awed into submission political bullies who controlled the elections." One of these was Judge Ned McGowan, prominent in the Broderick wing of California democracy, associate justice of the Court of Sessions, and involved in King's murder.

King had exposed McGowan as an ex-Philadelphia ballot-box expert with a criminal record in Pennsylvania. He was described as a gallant, shrewd, unscrupulous, jovial little blackguard, so thoroughly schooled in underworld politics that he had no difficulty "worming his way to prominence" in California.

"In morals and chivalry," said Major Bell, "Ned was emphatically an exaggerated edition of Aaron Burr."

He wore a tall white beaver and magnificent Magyar-like mustache just beginning to show the frost of many winters. In 1855 he rode at the zenith of his California prosperity.

The judge had formed a "convenient connection" with a blonde beauty of France, on whom he lavished his ardent affections and wealth in the way of high living, expensive wardrobe, jewelry, and a cottage on Pike Street worth $15,000. The blonde decided to have the house for herself, and "lavished her persuasive powers on her flexible lover" until the deed was signed and recorded, then told the judge to vamoose. When McGowan objected, her stalwart lover,

James King, editor of the *Bulletin* of San Francisco.

Surrender of Casey and Cora.

Vigilantes taking James Casey and Charles Cora from county jail to hang them in 1856.

Johnny Carpaud, appeared and offered an argument the judge couldn't resist. The blonde and Carpaud took over the love nest, and McGowan found lodging at the house of Madame Teresa Show on Dupont Street, only a block and a half from the cottage on Pike.

About four o'clock one afternoon the judge and some other tenants were in the front parlor engaged in a quiet game of poker when they heard a terrific explosion. Hurrying in the direction from which it came, they soon reached the love nest on Pike.

Several others already had arrived. Among them was Joe Stokes, apparently unconcerned about the whole matter.

Someone had sounded the fire alarm. The fire company arrived, but there was no need for its service. Someone had placed a huge petard beneath the window on the front porch and lighted the fuse. Johnny Carpaud had accidentally opened the door, spotted the sizzling explosive, snatched it up and tossed it toward the street. But it exploded as it left his hand, killing him instantly, and had so disfigured the cottage that even Judge McGowan didn't recognize it.

The affair produced a sensation. McGowan was arrested, but he was released when he proved that he was with the party in Madame Show's parlor when the bomb exploded. The identity of the perpetrator was not known until the following March.

McGowan had escaped the Vigilantes when they banished him from the state. Joe Stokes read the handwriting on the wall and headed for Nicaragua. Major Bell was a passenger on the same boat, and Joe confessed to him that it was he who had attempted to even Ned's score with the French blonde.

"I had a fight once in El Dorado," he said, "and killed a

man. They would have hanged me if it hadn't been for Judge
McGowan. I felt obligated to return the compliment at the
first opportunity."

He grinned and concluded: "You should have seen that
Johnny Carpaud when my petard exploded. I didn't think
there would be a piece left of him as big as a chew of
tobacco."

In Nicaragua, Joe fell in with a band of irregular military
adventurers involved in a revolution. With forty others, he
boarded the steamer *Cortez* to seize her for the Nicaraguan
government. The *Cortez* was commanded by Captain Napoleon Collins of the United States Navy, who captured Stokes
and the others and started for the United States. They
reached Panama at the outbreak of the bloody riot on April
6, 1856.

Nine hundred passengers from the steamer *Golden Gate*,
of San Francisco, about the same number from a New York
steamer, five hundred from a steamer from New Orleans, and
nearly four hundred from the *Cortez*, including passengers
from British steamers from the South America coast bound
for England, aggregating not less than three thousand, had
assembled at the railroad depot. Those on the Pacific side
were taking the train just vacated by the Eastern side passengers, who were boarding the *Golden Gate*.

A drunken Irishman, who had caused considerable trouble
on the steamer down from New York, got into an argument
with a native fruit vendor over a watermelon. The Irishman
insisted on taking the melon without paying. A fight started,
in which other natives took the part of their countryman, and
some of the passengers, ignorant of the cause, interfered in
behalf of the Irishman. The affair erupted into a general fight
with pistols and knives.

It was nearly sunset. The bells of Barrio de Santa Ana, a dirty suburb, brought its vagabond populace rushing to the depot. With cries of rage and defiance, the hoots and yells of the natives and the groans of dying men being cut to pieces mingling with the firing of guns and the smashing of doors and windows of the screaming locomotive trying to escape only half-filled with passengers, the fight burst into a riot.

The soldiers fell out in full force and raced to the scene with fixed bayonets. Someone seeing them running through the streets raised the cry, "Revolution! Revolution!" which was taken up and passed from door to door. There followed an instantaneous barricading of doors and windows and the firm refusal to admit even the screaming, crying women and children fleeing from the carnage.

Only two points of organized defense offered sanctuary for those able to escape the bloody pandemonium. One was the Aspinwall Hotel, set up by Ran Runnels, an American resident of Panama. Runnels was a man of great courage and influence, married to the governor's niece. A howling crowd of natives had barricaded the street at the Ocean House, a hundred yards from the depot. Brandishing their cutlasses, they demanded of the governor an order for arms from the government arsenal, which was refused. With a derringer thrust against their leader's stomach and a threat to "send an ounce of lead through the waistband of his pants" if his party was harmed, Runnels led his fighters through to safety of the Aspinwall. From there, companies of men handy with gun and knife were dispatched to attack the rear of the main body of the mob. They kept up their sorties during the night and returned each time with a large number of passengers. Thus several hundred panic-stricken persons were saved.

The second point of defense was the railroad baggage

room where hundreds of passengers, under the direction of Joe Stokes, had taken refuge when the fighting began. Few were armed. Those who carried guns had little or no extra ammunition. But they so guarded the one entrance to the room and securely barricaded themselves behind its thin walls that they could have held off the mob but for an unfortunate incident.

The soldiers, who arrived to disperse the attackers with bayonets, were mistaken for part of the mob and fired upon by the barricaded passengers. The soldiers returned the fire and joined the mob.

Joe Stokes defended the entrance throughout the night. While the passengers reloaded and passed revolvers to him, he repulsed charge after charge. About midnight he and Bob Marks, a watchman at the depot, set up an old swivel gun in the baggage room, loaded it to the muzzle with boiler rivets, and pointed it toward the door. At 3 A.M., when the passengers ran out of ammunition and shots ceased to come from within, the soldiers battered down the door and charged at bayonet.

Joe fired the battery. The blast knocked them off their feet, killing fifteen of them and wounding several more. They fell back, only for a moment, then charged again.

Joe and Bob Marks didn't wait to witness the effect of their "farewell." They fled upstairs into the telegraph room. Joe had just finished reloading his pistol when a soldier leaped through the doorway and shot him through the lungs. Bob Marks was bayoneted. The wounded below were brained, and except for the looting that followed, the Panama massacre had ended.

Colonel Garrido, a courageous and humane officer, arrived in time to stop the carnage in the baggage room. He heard the shot that killed Joe Stokes and rushed upstairs in time to prevent him from being bayoneted. He died in the colonel's arms.

Joe was the hero of the night. When the news reached San Francisco, a movement was begun to erect a monument to his heroic defense of the passengers of Panama. Unfortunately, the Vigilantes had branded him an outlaw, and the matter was dropped.

They buried Joe the next day. With the consent of the governor, Colonel Garrido ordered a platoon to fire a salute over his grave.

The colonel said: "Poor fellow! What I would have given to have saved him. He was the bravest man I ever saw."

Major Bell wrote: "He died the death of a hero and martyr, and deserved a monument."

6. Tangdhangtanka

The Osage Terror

THE Osage, a hilly, timbered section of northeastern Oklahoma, came into the national limelight following the Civil War. The government purchased it from the Cherokee Indians and herded the remnants of the once-proud Osage tribe into the reservation.

In that region anything can, and has, happened.

For years these hills, in places almost inaccessible, were the hideout of the Dalton and Starr gangs of territorial desperadoes. As late as 1923 they were overrun by the notorious Al Spencer gang of bandits.

Then the white man set up oil derricks. Black gold flowed from the earth in such quantity that this land of scrub-oak forests and red-clay loam became the country's greatest oil fields. Correspondingly, the Osages became the richest per capita nation in the world. Wealthy members of the tribe were slain for control of fabulous headrights.

But the weirdest drama played against this backdrop occurred in the early 1880's. It has been recorded as the "Osage Terror."

In July, 1883, Karl Fentwick, a New York man, came West for his health and settled his family in the northwest corner of the Osage reservation. A few weeks later he celebrated the birthday of his small daughter, Katie, with a feast and much merrymaking, and presented her with a valuable gold chain and locket of antique workmanship.

After dinner Katie went to play in the woods—and never returned. The alarmed father organized a searching party. They combed the woods for hours. But little Katie couldn't be found.

That night a severe storm uprooted trees and broiled streams from their banks. The next morning, with still no trace of little Katie, Fentwick gave her up as having been drowned. Her body was believed to have been swept away in one of the swollen creeks to the river.

In December George Bitters, a mail carrier, set out from Sedan, Kansas, for the town of Peru in the Osage Nation. He never arrived.

His horse was found in the timber, with saddle and bridle missing. But George Bitters had vanished.

The following spring Elmer Johnson went hunting in the hills and disappeared. His rifle was found with the stock broken. His hat lay nearby, covered with blood.

In September, 1885, a party of hunters came upon the skeletons of two horses and a weatherbeaten wagon that had been abandoned for at least a year. It contained the possessions of two men. But there was no trace of their bodies.

On February 12, 1886, Oscar Beach went hunting along the northern border of the reservation and vanished as mysteriously as the others.

A tense gloom, shot through with anger and suspicion, settled over the country. Even the Indians feared and distrusted one another. United States marshals were unable to solve the mystery.

Fentwick himself was convinced now that little Katie had become the victim of whatever had happened to the others, and the storm had not been the answer to his child's fate.

At the time a railroad being built across Kansas was extended south into the Osage. It was necessary to cut through a wild promontory called Cascade Hill. For this job the company shipped in a gang of Italian laborers. In charge was a powerfully built Irishman named Pat Durfee, who always wore a gold chain about his neck.

The first night in camp some of the crew complained that there had been a prowler in their tents. Pat Durfee laughed at their fears. But the molestations continued. Durfee decided he would sit up alone and trap the strange visitor.

About midnight he dozed. Suddenly he was awakened by something tugging at the chain around his neck. A shadowy figure dashed away in the moonlight.

Durfee whipped up his rifle and fired. The marauder fell in the brush, thrashing about and screaming like a wounded animal.

As Durfee approached for another shot, a huge man in fantastic garb of leather and skins leaped to his feet. His eyes shone and his nostrils were dilated in a spine-chilling look of savagery.

Before Durfee could fire a second shot, the man seized him in a mad embrace. One strong hand wielded a club. With a single blow he knocked Durfee unconscious. When the Irishman came to, his gold chain was missing.

Quickly he organized a posse. With three Indians as guides, they set out in pursuit. Blood spots on the ground showed that Durfee had wounded his attacker, apparently in the right leg.

They followed the trail all night and the next day. Late in the evening they entered a ravine in a wild, broken section of the hills so choked with jungle it was almost impenetrable. The trail ended at the mouth of a cave.

Without warning their quarry launched an attack. From an upthrust of rock above he hurled heavy stones with such unerring aim that the posse suffered three casualties before they could retreat. Durfee fired until his rifle was empty, without hitting the animal-like being.

As he attempted to reload, the figure leaped from the rocks and charged him, his screams echoing through the hills. Durfee clubbed his rifle, and the Italians drew their knives.

They struggled fiercely, finally smashing him to the ground, where he lay writhing and frothing at the mouth and shrieking in diabolical rage. A knife, plunged into his heart, ended his wild cries.

The Indian guides took one look at the man-animal's face and fled. The Italian laborers shuddered and Durfee gasped as they gazed down at the most horrible features they had ever seen.

The wild man's face was burned black and seamed with scars. The nose had been broken and had grown back horribly twisted. Where the upper lip had been torn away, broken teeth jutted like fangs. Shaggy hair was matted about his head and jaws. Around his wrists were heavy steel bands. From one still dangled a link of chain.

Inside the cave another ghastly sight met their eyes. On a shelf of rock, sixteen in all, sat an array of grinning skulls.

There was a crude fireplace, some cooking utensils, and a grass bed. Hanging from pegs driven in the wall were George Bitters' saddle and bridle and empty mail pouch, the clothing of Elmer Johnson, the gun of Oscar Beach, and many other items whose owners were never known.

Stuffed in a crevice with several other pieces of jewelry they found little Katie Fentwick's locket and the gold chain Pat Durfee had worn about his neck.

They identified the killer as Tangdhangtanka (the panther), a Delaware half-breed who had been placed in irons for his tribal crimes, escaped years before, and was thought to have died from exposure.

He lies buried in the ravine where he was captured and slain.

7. Ben Cravens

Lobo Killer

IN 1893 deputy United States marshals scoured the Kansas-Oklahoma Territory border for a man named Ben Cravens who peddled whisky to the Indians. A wily customer, he kept one jump ahead of them, until May, 1894, when he stole twenty head of cattle in the Osage Nation and sold them to a butcher at Perry, in the Cherokee Strip.

He was arrested at Caney, Kansas, and lodged in the Perry jail. But while awaiting trial, he effected his break and a wholesale delivery of prisoners. For the next decade he was the most elusive, and perhaps the most dangerous, outlaw to operate in the Southwest.

Cravens was an excellent shot with a rifle. His specialties were stock thievery and robbery of country stores and post offices—small compared with the train and bank holdups of the reckless bands of adventurers of the newly opened Oklahoma lands from which sprang the Starrs, the Daltons, and the Doolins. But his jobs were lucrative and filled with adventure. When cornered, he would escape in a running fight.

Usually, he chose as a companion some young fellow with little or no experience. When Cravens had no further use for him, he took charge of the loot and rode away. In one instance he blasted his companion with a Winchester and left him for dead.

This affair placed Cravens in the unprecedented position of being the only frontier bad man whose shoes, purchased for his wedding day, were worn to the penitentiary by his companion, who also was scheduled to be best man at his wedding, and for a crime they committed to secure funds to defray expenses of the honeymoon.

Cravens grew up on a farm in Iowa, a terror to his teachers and to the pupils. One night he broke all the windows of the schoolhouse in revenge for a severe licking he had received for bad behavior. He was placed in jail, but escaped, and fled to the Kansas frontier.

Elgin, Kansas, was the principal shipping point for cattle herds coming out of the Osage, Cherokee, and Creek Nations of the Indian Territory, and one of the wildest towns on the border in the late 1880's. The "festal array" of the cowboy appealed to the fancy of this unsophisticated, awkward boy of fifteen, and ranch life seemed the fulfillment of all his boyish dreams.

For a while he worked as a cowboy in the Osage and Creek Nations, becoming familiar with the country and forming many acquaintances. But it soon became monotonous to ride the same line day after day.

There were easier ways of making a living, quicker methods of making a fortune. The Indian Territory was "short on enforcement of law, but long on cattle and horses that could be marketed without consent of the owners." And the Indians wanted whisky.

Cravens stole horses, peddled whisky, served a short sentence in the federal jail at Guthrie in 1894, then turned to cattle rustling, which landed him in jail at Perry. After his escape, he was reputed to have engaged in numerous robberies in the Territory. But officers were never able to capture him.

When hard pressed, Cravens would cross the Kansas line, stay in the sunflower state until his trail cooled, then return to his old haunts and habits. In November, 1896, he held up the store of Hooper & Tweedy, at Hewins, in Chautauqua County, Kansas, took $350 in cash and merchandise, stole a horse from Fred Gaddie, who was a customer in the store, and fled back to Oklahoma.

In the Cherokee Strip he teamed up with a wild lad named Dan Clifton, alias Dynamite Dick, one of the survivors of the Doolin gang. Clifton had been one of fifteen prisoners who had escaped from the federal jail at Guthrie in July of that year, under the leadership of Bill Doolin. He was known to have been in eight bank and train robberies with Bill Doolin and the Daltons, and suspected of many other crimes. He and Cravens decided to rob the bank at Blackwell.

They rode into town the morning of December 3, examined the surroundings and location of the bank. They decided to rob it the next day. They bought some supplies and rode east.

A liveryman recognized Cravens and notified Sheriff A. O. Lund. Lund and Deputy M. Dossi organized a posse and picked up the trail of the outlaws. At three o'clock the next morning they located them at a deserted cabin in the woods three miles east of Blackwell. They surrounded the hideout and waited until daylight.

Ben Cravens, lobo killer.

At dawn the outlaws discovered they were surrounded by armed men. Cravens decided to adopt his old tactics and make a running fight for the woods.

The two outlaws sprang into the open, firing rapidly. Clifton ran forty yards before he was brought down with a shot through the heart from Sheriff Lund's Winchester. Cravens fell near the cabin, shot twice through the body and lungs.

Coughing and bleeding at the mouth, he was laid in a wagon and hauled into Blackwell. He refused to confess his partner's identity and made no statement concerning their activities. To the surprise of everyone he recovered. He was returned to Kansas, convicted of robbery of the store in Chautauqua County, and sentenced to twenty years in the state penitentiary at Lansing.

In prison, Cravens was assigned to a coal-mining gang, and became acquainted with a notorious bank robber and life termer named E. F. Estelle. On the morning of November 16, 1897, they fell into step with their fellow prisoners as usual and were taken to the mines several hundred feet underground. When the prisoners had been distributed to the tunnels, Cravens and Estelle stalked back through the darkness and overpowered the guard at the hoisting shaft.

Armed with the guard's revolver and rifle, they entered the car and forced him to give the hoisting signal. As the car started upward, they caved in his head with a pick handle and dumped his body back into the shaft.

The spot of daylight above came closer. They reached the surface and paused, momentarily blinded by the bright sunlight. It was long enough for the outside guards to realize they were prisoners attempting a break. Leaving Estelle to shift for himself, Cravens dashed madly through the cordon of men, shooting as he ran.

Both escaped. Estelle went north to Kansas City. He was recaptured two years later in Tennessee and returned to northern Illinois, where he was wanted for a daring holdup near Quincy. Cravens stole a horse and fled to his old haunts and the scenes of his first depredations.

At the time he was sentenced to the penitentiary he had owned several head of cattle. These had been left with a farmer near the Otoe reservation to dispose of, and it is believed that it was to collect his money that Cravens returned to Oklahoma.

In his escape from prison he had been struck in the head by a bullet that had lodged under his scalp. He was suffering from the wound when he reached the home of Joe Webb, near Red Rock.

Webb wanted to call a doctor, but Cravens refused. He commanded the farmer to cut out the bullet himself. Webb feared Cravens, and with a razor he carved the lead from the outlaw's scalp, applied some home remedy, and the wound soon healed.

Cravens took a job shucking corn, and though his presence in the Otoe country was known to many, and a reward of $2,000 was offered for his capture, no one had the temerity to claim it. He had too many friends in the area to be taken unawares by officers.

Several times the officials were notified of his whereabouts. But they were never able to find him. One man, particularly vigilant in assisting officers in their search in the daytime, shared Cravens' bed at night.

That winter Cravens fell in love. The gallantry of the outlaw and his persistency in courtship finally gained the young woman's consent to marriage, and the ceremony was set for early April.

The bride-to-be was busy with her trousseau. Cravens ordered his wedding suit and purchased a new pair of shoes. He still needed funds for expenses of the wedding and honeymoon.

With him at the time was a youth named Bert Welty, who had been attracted to Cravens through a desire for the outlaw life. The matter was discussed between them, and they decided to rob the store of Swartz & Company at Red Rock. Swartz was a trader among the Ponca, Otoe, and Tonkawa Indians, and kept considerable cash.

On the night of March 10 Welty rigged himself in a woman's dress and sunbonnet, and Cravens disguised himself as a cowboy. Welty owned only a pair of heavy felt boots for wear with the dress, and he borrowed Cravens' wedding shoes. They secured a wagon, hitched their saddle horses to it, and drove to their destination.

It was dark when they arrived. A storm was brewing. They left their outfit in the timber outside of town and hurried toward the store on foot, carrying their rifles.

Several people were in the store as the bandits entered. They were successful in securing $1,200 from the customers and the store vault, and would have escaped in safety had not Welty, desiring a chew, stepped behind the counter for a plug of tobacco.

At that moment Alvin Bateman, the manager, grabbed up a pistol and fired, wounding Welty critically. Cravens opened fire from the doorway, killing Bateman instantly. As Bateman fell, Welty staggered from behind the counter, shooting him through the body as he passed over him. Cravens helped

Welty through the doorway with the sack of loot, and they fled to their wagon.

The storm broke. Thunder rumbled, lightning jagged the heavens, and rain poured in torrents. In the darkness, Cravens guided the team into a gulch and broke down the wagon.

Cravens stripped the harness off the team, and began to saddle the horses. Welty struggled up from the wreckage with the sack of money. Cravens had no further use for him now. He lifted his gun and discharged it in the young bandit's face. Welty fell back in the mud, blood running from his cheek and neck.

Unable to see distinctly in the darkness with the rain beating down, Cravens thought he had blown off the youth's head. He picked up the money, mounted one horse, and leading the other, disappeared in the night.

Welty had been shot through the side of the face. He regained consciousness and made his way ten miles up Black Bear Creek to the home of a farmer named Charles Heatherington. Heatherington summoned a doctor, and cared for Welty until Sheriff George Foster and his posse arrived from Perry and placed him under arrest.

Welty was tried in federal court for the murder of Bateman because the crime had been committed on an Indian reservation. Cravens' sweetheart was the chief government witness against him, and he went to the United States penitentiary at Fort Leavenworth for life wearing Cravens' shoes.

Deputy Sheriff Jean Branson of Perry rode to Red Rock the night of the killing. At daybreak he picked up Cravens' trail in the mud and followed the tracks of the two horses to the home of a farmer named Isom Cunningham, three miles northwest of Pawnee. The two horses stood in Cunningham's corral.

At Pawnee, Branson enlisted the aid of Sheriff John Crismon and deputies Tom Johnson and Joe Weariman. The officers rode to Cunningham's farm, called him from the house, and asked if Cravens was there.

The farmer denied that he had seen the outlaw. Deputy Johnson, doubting this, dismounted and walked across the yard. He was in the open about ten feet from the front door when Cravens pushed it open with the muzzle of his rifle and fired.

His first shot struck Johnson in the abdomen. His second shot tore into Sheriff Crismon's wrist, shattering his gunstock. Then Cravens leaped from the door, running, heading for the timber eighty yards across a plowed field.

Branson and Weariman were both good shots. They sprayed lead after him, but he jumped over a bank into a ravine and escaped without being hit.

Deputy Johnson died at Pawnee that night, and word went out to officers everywhere to find Ben Cravens.

It seemed that the killer had taken a back track into Noble County, where he stole a horse and saddle from a German farmer near Lela, then headed east again into the Creek Nation. The posse tracked him to the border of the Creek Indian country, but lost his trail on the frozen ground.

For weeks afterward they watched Cravens' sweetheart. From Catoosa, in the Cherokee Nation, he wrote to her under an assumed name, stating that he would remain there until he received an answer. She was to outline to him all that she heard as to plans for his capture.

The letter was read by federal officials before it was permitted to reach her. Several officers, together with a man who knew Cravens, were stationed in the post office to arrest him when he called for his mail.

The acquaintance was to step up to him with the purpose of shaking hands, then gripping the outlaw's hands until the officers could overpower him. But Cravens' instinct was quick. As the friend sought to grip his hand, he jerked away, darted through the rear door, and leaped toward the brush that skirted the town on the south.

The officers opened fire, emptying their weapons before he reached the brush, but Cravens escaped again unscathed. In the brush they found the horse and saddle he had stolen from the German farmer.

For the next five years Cravens was sought throughout the Southwest. He was accused of every crime in the country where the perpetrator was not identified or apprehended. Rewards aggregating $10,000 were placed on his head.

These were for known crimes he had committed. The government wanted him for the murder of Alvin Bateman; the Territory of Oklahoma wanted him for the murder of Deputy Sheriff Johnson, and the state of Kansas sought him for the murder of a prison guard.

Numerous tales sprang up as to his activities. In the Oklahoma Territory, people delighted in telling how he taunted officers by appearing "under their very noses" in Guthrie, Oklahoma City, and other points, even adding the luxury of intoxication and frequently remaining overnight in some saloon.

Some claimed that for more than a year after the murder of Johnson, Cravens traveled throughout Texas, New Mexico, and Arizona as a salesman, faultlessly attired, a sauve conversationalist, carrying an important commercial line.

Others said he was basking quietly in Old Mexico. Masquerading as a scion of the family of a prominent Pennsylvania governor, he had appeared at an American colony in

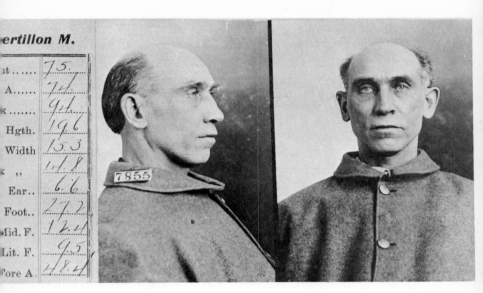

Photos of Ben Cravens with Bertillon measurements which helped establish his identity after he entered Missouri prison as Charles Maust.

the city of Guadalojano with plenty of money, a well-trimmed Vandyke beard, and dressed in fashion. His advent had caused a sensation among the ladies of the colony, but the pretty daughter of a wealthy mineowner had won his attention and married him, and had borne him a son.

Every report was checked. Several officers in Oklahoma resigned positions to which they had been elected to trail and capture Ben Cravens for the fabulous price on his head. But the outlaw had disappeared completely. He was almost forgotten.

Then up in Missouri a man named Charles Maust hired out as a farm hand. He married a local girl and settled down to a respectable, honest life.

Finally his old propensities crept out. He stole a horse, and was sentenced to four years in the state penitentiary. A few days after his arrival at Jefferson City, a barber, who had been in Lansing prison with Cravens, recognized Maust and notified prison officials.

Fervently Maust denied that he was the notorious outlaw, and that he had never seen the barber before in his life. But Bertillon records sent from the Kansas prison agreed in every detail.

He was brought to Guthrie by the federal government. In November, 1911, he went on trial in the United States District Court for the murder of Alvin Bateman. Numerous witnesses identified Maust as Cravens, and Bert Welty, brought from the penitentiary, made a full confession.

On January 29, 1912, Ben Cravens was sentenced to serve the rest of his life in the federal prison at Fort Leavenworth.

8. Bill Pickett

The Man Who Invented Bulldogging

IN the early days of Wild West shows and rodeos, when all America was cheering Buffalo Bill, Pawnee Bill, Annie Oakley, J. Ellison Carrol, and many others, none was more colorful and spectacular than the daredevil half-breed cowboy from the Miller brothers' fabulous 101 Ranch of Oklahoma, Bill Pickett, who originated the event which became one of the top attractions of today's rodeo—bulldogging.

He would chase the longhorn on his pony until the horse reached the steer's side, then leap from the saddle to the head and horns, and stop the animal by digging his heels in the ground. Using the horns for levers, he would twist the steer's neck until the nose was pointing upward. Then Pickett would sink his teeth into the animal's tender lip, bulldog fashion, turn loose all holds, and topple backward. The tenderness of the lip brought the animal over on its side.

This biting of the steer's lip gave the trick the name it

Bill Pickett on Spradley, the horse he used in his famous bull-dogging exploit in Mexico City's bull ring.

carried even after other cowboys learned they could throw the animal by hanging onto its horns alone and wrestling it down.

Pickett was an employee of the 101 and its Wild West shows from the turn of the century until the great ranch disintegrated in the 1930's. During that time nearly every bone in his body was broken. But neither broken bones nor painful injuries dampened his enthusiasm or ability in his chosen sport. He was the only man in the history of bull-fighting who ever handled, barehanded and unaided, a Spanish bull.

This event occurred in Mexico City before a crowd of twenty-five thousand. He won $53,000 in thirty-eight minutes, and had it not been for the protection of the Mexican rurales, he probably would never have lived to enjoy it.

Pickett was a strapping cowboy whose mother was a full-blood Choctaw and father a mixture of white, Indian, and Negro. Before joining the 101, he had spent several years on ranches in South America, Texas, and New Mexico. He was a tremendous attraction at any kind of celebration, being the only cowboy bulldogger, and many were the stories of his reckless daring with man-killing horses and wild, murderous cattle.

Once at an El Paso fair he had been pitted against a furious elk. Its great sweep of snaggy, bladed horns would have killed him with a single blow. Pickett wrestled and threw the huge animal in less than ten minutes and emerged unscathed. It became the belief in the Southwest that the four-footed beast that could beat him in a standup fight had not been born, and with this conviction the Miller brothers invaded Mexico.

Pickett's mad scamper on horseback after a Texas steer,

his midair leap from the saddle onto the flying horns of the fleeing quarry, and his struggle and inevitable overturning of the animal were new to the Mexicans. It was the only American performance even remotely similar to their beloved bullfighting. The bullfighters, who came in a group one afternoon to witness the exhibition of daredeviltry, laughed contemptuously.

That night, at the Café Colon, rendezvous of the bullfighters and their admirers, Colonel Joe Miller, who owned half interest in the show, placed bets two to one that no member of their fraternity would dare duplicate the feat. Bienvenida, noted for his eye and stroke, and as deadly a matador as Mexico ever produced, accepted the challenge. The following morning the Mexican *Herald* and other native newspapers announced that he would be on the scene promptly at ten o'clock "to teach the boasting Americans a lesson in grace and courage."

Bienvenida failed to show up, and sent no word of explanation or apology. While scores of guests waited and wondered, Miller dispatched a messenger to his hotel. There lolled Bienvenida, "languidly regretful" that the men of the bull ring who held him under contract had forbidden such a risk of his precious neck.

This should have satisfied Joe Miller. But the showman's Americanism was running rampant. Publicly he charged Bienvenida with showing the white feather.

That evening at the Café Colon he proposed to Señor Louis F. Correra of the *Herald* and the astonished bullfighters to match Pickett, barehanded and without assistance, against the most blood-hungry bull turned into the arena— for the gate receipts and $5,000. And Pickett had not even been consulted!

To the Mexicans the execution of such a proposal meant sure death to the cowboy. Obviously Miller was not familiar with bull-ring procedure.

A bullfighter relied upon his quickness of eye and remarkable agility in evading the furious assaults of his maddened antagonist. The *picadors,* mounted on worthless, blindfolded horses, received the first charges of the bull with lances. When the bull had been aroused to fury, the *picadors* were replaced by the *chulos,* with *banderillas,* or barbed darts, which they drove into the beast's shoulders until the bull became weakened from loss of blood, fierce and bewildered.

Then the matador entered with his piece of scarlet silk and naked sword. As the bull's eye caught the silk and he rushed blindly, the matador stepped nimbly aside and plunged the sword into his spine to end the affair. The red cloth, which the bull was taught from infancy to detest, was the object of attack. The matador performed at a distance. He did not dare even lay hands on the bull.

That Miller's cowboy, Pickett, would engage such an animal in hand-to-hand combat "set the gay Mexican capital agog."

Miller did not bet that Pickett could throw the animal. He knew the necks of these bulls were too thick to twist them down. But he bet that Pickett could grab one of them by the horns and stay with the animal five minutes.

Bullfight promotion officials accepted the challenge with the stipulation that Pickett stay in the arena for fifteen minutes, five of which were to be spent on the animal's head, and the Mexicans, sure that the bull would shake loose the cowboy in a matter of seconds and then gore him to death, eagerly covered the bet.

Much publicity was given the daring of this half-breed

cowboy. Thousands of spectators, including President Por-
firio Díaz and other ranking Mexican officials and nobility,
turned out to see him "sacrifice himself upon the altar of
American egotism." Gate receipts for the day totaled $48,000,
making the total wager $53,000.

Miller agreed that Señor Rivero, impresario to El Toreo,
the new concrete and steel bull ring where the encounter
was to take place, would select the animal. Rivero chose
Bonito, a fierce, big black bull that already had killed two
men and a half-dozen horses but had been spared the death
thrust at the entreaties of spectators that such a brave, strong
bull should not die so ingloriously, and he had been returned
to the corrals to await his next challenger.

Miller and the Wild West troupe escorted Pickett to the
arena. Señor Rivero and the presidente, Señor Bravo, received them with apprehension. They confessed to Miller
that they had believed Pickett would lose courage at the last
moment and fail to appear.

"The cowboy was never more confident and eager for a
fray," Miller said later. "He was actually grinning as he
watched the crowd pouring into the enclosure."

Then, at the last moment, orders came from the governor
of the federal district to stop the battle. A group of American
women in the city, in the name of humanity, had protested
the affair that could end only in the death of this "rash
Oklahoman." They had enlisted the aid of American officials
and businessmen whose influence had forced the governor
to revoke the permit.

The bull-ring managers were about to announce the can-
cellation, but Joe Miller insisted:

"The governor has forbidden Pickett to fight only Bonito.
You have other bulls as savage. Pickett will meet any one of

them you choose."

And while the delegation of women were at home con-
gratulating themselves, a new license was handed the impresario and presidente.

Señor Rivero now selected Frijoli Chiquita (Little Beans).
Little Beans was a beautiful animal, almost dark purple in
color, and his short, thick neck was more powerful looking
than Bonito's. This was much to the satisfaction of the experienced impresario, for upon the neck and horns Pickett
would exert his strength—if ever he succeeded in getting
hold of the beast. Like Bonito, he already had killed several
horses and men. His reputation for courage and savage fighting ability matched that of Bonito's.

But down in the arena a huge board had been displayed
to the crowd with the following announcement in Spanish:
"By request, Bonito has been withdrawn and another bull
substituted."

It implied that Miller and his troupe, fearing Bonito's
prowess, had made the request. The crowd jeered. They
quieted down somewhat when Miller ran in a second sign
stating that Bonito would not appear because of the governor's order, and that Frijoli Chiquita was perhaps an even
more formidable opponent.

Miller had planned to present his whole Wild West performance, climaxing it with the fight between Pickett and
the bull. But the lust for blood and battle was upon the
25,000 hostile Mexicans demanding "El feroz fenomeno
negro de Oklahoma!"

Miller was not foolish enough to antagonize such a mob.
He withdrew his performers at once, and announced the
"Gran Lucka Taurina-Humana."

Obviously Pickett had underestimated the danger he

faced. His victories in the Southwest had made him over-confident, and up to this moment he had likened the bellowing Spanish monsters to a fighting Texas steer. As the 101's publicity agent, W. C. Thompson, who reported the event to American newspapers, aptly expressed it: "Frijoli Chiquita's size and proclivities were as much like his bovine American brothers as a wildcat and a chipmunk."

While the cowboy was saddling his favorite horse, Spradley, and getting a lot of worthless advice from his companions, a half-dozen El Toreo vaqueros were torturing the bull to man-killing fury. Tension mounted among the thousands waiting in the hot Mexican sun.

There were boos and hisses as Bill Pickett entered the arena. There was tumultuous shouting and applause as a gate swung open and Frijoli Chiquita blasted into that sun to kill. Finding himself face to face with the dusky cowboy and his horse, he put down his head as if taking aim, and charged furiously toward them.

Pickett, realizing his peril, sucked air through his teeth and his face paled. Then his nerves steadied, his muscles tensed for the onslaught. So did his cow horse Spradley. From long experience on the prairie Spradley was wise to the moods and ways of the wildest cattle. He stood with his feet wide in the sand, his rump pinched gracefully, as the bull bore down on them.

The crowd screamed in crescendo, for it looked as though the horns couldn't miss. But when the sharp points were within twenty feet of Spradley, the horse jumped sideways. The bull, thinking the target was escaping, veered off his course to intercept it. In that split second Spradley jumped in the opposite direction, and as the bull swept past, he planted his hind hoofs solidly into the beast's side.

The momentum carried the bull nearly fifteen feet past the horse, but he recovered and wheeled and charged back so suddenly that there was no time to organize a second defense. His needle-pointed horns drove into Spradley's shoulder. As they came out, covered with blood, Pickett leaped between them and grasped the bull around the neck.

This was the moment awaited by the 25,000 spectators. If Pickett should secure a hold on the bull, he would never keep it, the experts had said. One toss of the bull's head would send him flying to the ground. Within a matter of seconds he would be dead. The El Toreo was on the verge of becoming a cage of howling maniacs.

Thompson reported: "It looked as if every man, woman, and child was on his or her feet, straining for a clear view of the gruesome spectacle the Mexican mind had fondly pictured. Not a sound they uttered, but a concentrated paean of wild exultation was waiting on their lips.

"But down in the arena the unexpected—no, the supposedly impossible—was happening. The dreaded bull was frantically tossing his head with all his great strength, bellowing his rage and bewilderment, pirouetting in dizzy circles, and there still dangled Pickett—his bearlike hug unshaken, and he clinging like a burr. How infantile the strength, how clumsy the skill, how feeble the courage of the adored toreadors in comparison with the exhibition being given by this hated stranger from the north!

"Not only could the bull not toss or trample or otherwise harm his antagonist, but the cowboy actually had the beast tottering on his feet. The haughty, shaggy head was aslant under the force exerted by the swinging man upon the horns. The hold was Pickett's favorite and never before had a four-footed creature withstood it."

The largest diversified Farm and Ranch in the United States.

BLISS, OKLAHOMA.

THE FINEST HERD OF
Buffalo
IN EXISTENCE

BUFFALO
FOR
SALE.

1:30 p. m.	**GRAND PARADE**
	Indians, Cowboys, Prairie Schooners, Ox Wagons, Oklahoma Farmers, Modern Farm Machinery, Steam Plow, Automobiles, 12 Bands.
2:15 p. m.	**BUFFALO CHASE.**
2:30 p. m.	**INDIAN SPORTS AND DANCES.**

2:50 p. m.	MISS LUCILE MULHALL and HER HORSE, "GOVERNOR." MR. GEO. ELSER, Champion Trick Rider of the World.
3:20 p. m.	RIDING WILD BRONCOS.
4:00 p. m.	CHAMPION STEER ROPING CONTEST.
4:45 p. m.	THE WONDERFUL NEGRO "PICKETT." Throwing Wild Steer by the Nose with His Teeth.
5:00 p. m.	COWBOYS AND GIRLS IN HORSEBACK QUADRILLE.
5:15 p. m.	BURNING EMIGRANT WAGON TRAIN BY INDIANS.
5:30 p. m.	RECEPTION BY THE INDIANS.

"Home, Sweet Home."

SADDLES USED ON 101 RANCH MADE BY R. T. FRAZIER, PUEBLO, COLO.

F. P. BURNAP STATIONERY & PRINTING CO.,
KANSAS CITY, MO.

Menu of Events of the 101 Ranch Wild West Show. Note item at 4:45 p.m., "THE WONDERFUL NEGRO 'PICKETT'" Throwing Wild Steer by the Nose with His Teeth."

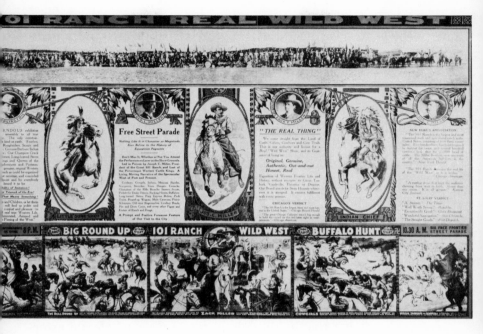

Program of 101 Ranch Wild West Show. For thirty years Bill Pickett worked for the fabulous 101 Ranch, doing his part in bringing wealth and fame to the Miller Brothers and winning a permanent niche for himself in the rodeo hall of fame as "The Dusky Demon."

The minutes ticked away while Pickett hung on grimly. Angry shouts swept through the grandstand. Someone cried in Spanish: "Remember Bienvenida!" A cushion was hurled into Pickett's face.

The act was hailed with uproarious applause, and a fusillade of the canvas missiles followed. This terminated with shouts of delight from the spectators. Someone threw a stone, and blood streamed down from the cowboy's cut face. Then hell broke loose.

The crowd shouted insults and howled for Pickett's blood. Fruits, bottles, canes, and knives showered the cowboy as he battled the blood-hungry bull. The Mexican *Record* next day ran a photograph of the litter covering the arena ground, and a picture in *El Imparcial,* the government publication, showed Pickett trying to dodge the missiles and at the same time maintain his hold on the bull to keep from being gored to death. And no one in the crowd raised a finger to stop it.

The show troupe appealed to the police. The police only laughed. The cowboys asked Miller for permission to open up on the mob with Winchesters and six-shooters, but Miller realized that that could only result in their wholesale extermination.

Another missile struck Pickett on the arm, and as the cowboy looked up into the hate of the crowd, his eyes filled with tears.

He was weakening fast. He tried to work the bull toward the barricade. But how could he turn it loose and reach safety ahead of those needle-pointed horns?

Miller shouted to Vester Pegg, a cowboy: "Take off your red shirt! Get over that wall. The moment Pickett turns loose of that bull, wave the garment in his face."

He ordered other members of the troupe to positions

where they could attract the bull's attention. It was a danger-ous assignment for them, but all were anxious to save the life of their comrade.

They had taken action none too soon. Their watches showed that Pickett had battled the storm of missiles and held the animal for thirty-eight minutes, seven and a half of which he had spent on its head, and Mexican temper had reached a fever pitch.

A brick thrown from the stands struck Pickett on the head. With a groan and a last, imploring look at his friends, he released his grip on the bull.

Pickett squirmed on the sand almost under the bull's nose. Frijoli Chiquita lowered his horns for the death thrust. The Mexicans yelled their delight.

Over the wall leaped the half-naked Vester Pegg, waving the hated color, red. The bull glimpsed it even before the astonished spectators did. For a moment he hesitated, then ran across Pickett's body and charged the insolent cowboy.

Pegg easily beat him to the wall and leaped to safety. Pickett staggered to his feet and ran stumbling to the barri-cade, where he was hauled to safety by Joe Miller. Frijoli Chiquita "pawed the earth and bellowed his impotent rage to an empty arena."

Later, Pickett returned to salute the presidente, a proce-dure necessary to collect the money. His second appearance in the ring so incensed the crowd that President Díaz, fear-ing that the cowboy might be lynched, ordered his rurales to escort the show troupe back to their grounds.

There were small demonstrations that night, but Mexican hatred soon abated. Joe Miller publicly offered $10,000 to any toreador who could duplicate Pickett's feat, but found no takers. The show returned to the United States a few days later, with the "patriotic satisfaction of knowing all Mexico could not put forward a man so intrepidly brave as this dusky Oklahoma half-breed gladiator."

Years afterward the southern republic still angrily discussed the event, and for more than a quarter century the 101 Ranch in Oklahoma was the top tourist attraction of the Southwest. Its famed White House played host to personalities from every walk of life, from United States Presidents and foreign diplomats to common cowboys. Its guest book read like a Who's Who in America.

Although the biting angle of bulldogging went out of style and became plain steer wrestling, Pickett continued to accompany the Wild West show on its tours, always ready to demonstrate his method and do his part in bringing wealth and fame to Colonel Joe Miller, Colonel George L. Miller, and Colonel Zack T. Miller and their vast ranch empire—a dream come true for their father, Colonel George W. Miller.

In so doing Pickett won a permanent niche for himself in the rodeo hall of fame as "The Dusky Demon." The sobriquet stuck to him the rest of his life. When the show closed and the ranch began to disintegrate in the early 1930's, he bought a quarter section of land eight miles from Chandler, Oklahoma, to become a modest rancher. The chief attraction in his corrals was his war horse Spradley with a great scar on his shoulder, a reminder of his Mexican venture.

But he was not content away from the 101. He returned to the ranch in 1932, at the age of seventy-one. Joe and George Miller were dead. Zack was sick in bed and the property was plastered with mortgages and threatened with foreclosure. Zack had some horses that were not subject to foreclosure and wanted them cut out of the herd before the rest went up for auction. Pickett agreed to do the job himself.

One big sorrel kept dodging back and forth at the far end
of the corral. When Pickett finally roped him, the animal
reared wildly and fell over backward. Pickett hauled him to
his feet, and as the horse stood still, dazed for a moment, the
cowboy started up the rope, hand over hand, toward him.

In his concern for his sick friend, Pickett forgot the danger
of his position. The horse snorted and reared high, chopping
at Pickett with his forefeet. Pickett dodged back, but too late.
One of the hoofs knocked him down, then the sorrel pounced
on him, with deadly hammer blows smashing at his chest and
head.

They picked up the cowboy and carried him to his bunk.
A doctor was called, but Pickett was beyond all help. His
skull had been crushed. A few minutes later he was dead.

His funeral services were conducted on the White House
porch, and he was buried on the ranch where he had spent
thirty turbulent years of his life.

9. Payne and Couch

Boomer Raiders

IN 1875 a man in Wichita, Kansas, was attracting as much attention on the frontier as the famous marshal, Wyatt Earp. People called him "Oklahoma Dave" Payne.

He had been born David Lewis Payne, in Grant County, Indiana, on December 30, 1836. His mother was a first cousin of the celebrated Davy Crockett, for whom he was named, and from whom he seemed to have inherited a character which led him into similar exploits on the Western frontier.

In 1875 he was in the prime of life. Of large, powerful frame, dressed in dark clothes, wearing a big black hat from under which curled long, wavy hair, and with a mustache and goatee, he presented a commanding appearance. Unlike most heroes of the plains, Payne was strictly a temperate man, so unlike the desperado and bravado in manners and deportment that he was immediately recognized as a dignified gentleman and esteemed as one of the most popular of men linked with the settlement of the West.

He had started west from Indiana with his brother in 1858 to engage in the Mormon war, which was then creating a furore throughout the country. By the time he reached Doniphan County, Kansas, the excitement had subsided, so he preempted a body of land there and erected a sawmill. This investment proved a poor venture, and Payne found himself without means.

At that time Doniphan County was the grazing grounds of buffalo, antelope, and other wild animals. Hunting these afforded a congenial outlet for his courageous heart and craving for adventure. He became so successful that he spread his operations into the mountains of New Mexico. He explored the course of the Cimarron River through the Indian Territory, and grew so familiar with the topography of the Southwest that he was in demand as a scout for the government and private expeditions and intimate with such distinguished guides and trappers as Kit Carson, Wild Bill, Buffalo Bill, and California Joe.

At the outbreak of the Civil War, Payne was one of the first to leave with the Fourth Regiment of Kansas Volunteers. This regiment was subsequently consolidated with the Third, and finally the two joined with the Tenth. Attached to the army of the frontier under General James G. Blunt, he engaged in nearly all the memorable conflicts that took place in Missouri and Arkansas.

In the battle of Prairie Grove, December 7, 1862, Payne distinguished himself for gallantry in action when he rescued his first lieutenant, Cyrus Leland, who had been badly wounded in the fierce onslaught against the enemy. Six times he was offered a commission, and six times he refused, because he "preferred to remain a private comrade with his friends."

After three years' service he returned to Doniphan County, and in the fall of 1864 was elected to the Kansas legislature. But before the legislative session began, General Sterling Price moved northward through Missouri with his fast-traveling Confederate army, and Payne was called upon to accept a captaincy in the Kansas militia to expel the invader. In the battle of Westport in September, 1864, Price withdrew, and Payne returned to his legislative duties, serving in the session of 1864–65.

Although never achieving the fame of an orator, he wielded strong influence for a first-session man. He spoke out of turn only once when a special bounty act was proposed. Payne opposed it vigorously on the grounds that Kansas already had exceeded her quota under all requisitions and could meet any additional demands in the service without bribing her volunteers. Too, granting bounties to future volunteers was discrimination against the soldiers who had freely enlisted.

"I have served three years as a private soldier without bounty," he said, "and I am ready to enlist upon the same terms as soon as the legislature adjourns."

The bill was defeated by an overwhelming vote.

When the legislature adjourned, Payne again volunteered for military service as a substitute for a poor neighbor who had been drafted and whose household full of children would have fallen upon the charity of the neighborhood.

The division to which Payne was attached was detailed for duty at Washington, where service was "little more than strict observance of methodical military punctilios." Every soldier was resplendent in white gloves, nobby uniforms with brilliant buttons, highly polished boots, and "their guns were required to shine like the armor of de Abigail, the ladies' knight-errant."

Captain David L. Payne.

This wasn't for the adventurous Dave Payne. He was back in Kansas in November, 1867, working at his occupation of plainsman, hunting and guarding caravan trains. He gained the respect of the wild Indians of the plains, and earned himself the title of "Cimarron Scout."

During the Indian outbreaks in western Kansas in 1868, he raised a company and was commissioned by Governor Crawford as captain of Company D, Eighteenth Kansas Cavalry. His regiment was sent to Camp Supply in the Indian Territory, attached to the command of Lieutenant General George A. Custer.

He participated in the winter campaign against the Cheyenne, Arapaho, and Kiowas in the western part of Indian Territory and the Texas panhandle. Although he fought several engagements with the hostiles, he was absent at the massacre of Black Kettle's camp of Cheyennes on the Washita. A few days later he accompanied General Sheridan's troops to the scene and helped bury Major Elliott and his men, who had been surrounded and killed by the Indians.

Early in 1869, when General Sheridan established a new post at Fort Sill on the eastern base of the Wichita Mountains so that his troops could operate from nearer the center of hostile territory, Payne conducted many hazardous scouts from the post with Wild Bill and California Joe. He became familiar with the Unassigned Lands, called Oklahoma, and at once realized the resources and possibilities of founding on this great domain a new American commonwealth.

Captain Payne moved to Sedgwick County, Kansas. His reputation preceded him. Though he was a Democrat, and the county was largely Republican, he was chosen to represent that district in the legislature in the session of 1871–72.

Through his influence, Sedgwick County was divided, and

a new county formed of the northern part called Harvey. In the redistricting of Sedgwick County, one of its largest townships was named "Payne" in his honor. In this township Payne made his new home, ten miles northeast of Wichita.

In 1872 he made a bid for the Senate, but was defeated. He moved to Newton to turn over a new leaf. Again he was well liked and respected, but through a hocus-pocus of money matters he lost all his properties. In 1875 he was back in Wichita, his eyes turned toward Washington, and securing testimonials and recommendations from powerful politicians such as General Tom Ewing, John J. Ingalls, and Preston B. Plumb, with whom he had allied himself, for a position as an officer in the United States House of Representatives.

He was appointed assistant doorkeeper. These duties afforded him the opportunity to investigate the conditions of various treaties made by the government with the Indians to 1866, by which the Oklahoma lands were ceded to the government and afterward surveyed for relocation of the Plains tribes and Negro freedmen. Payne claimed the right of white settlement, and thereafter became a thorn in the side of the government and the wealthy cattle companies using these lands to pasture their herds.

Through Payne's efforts the first large colony of "boomers" assembled on Bitter Creek on the border of the Indian Territory in December, 1880, for the purpose of entering the Oklahoma lands. They were met by federal cavalry under the command of Colonel J. J. Coppinger, with orders from the president that any attempt to enter the Indian Territory would be forcibly resisted.

Organizing military fashion, the colonists moved along the line to Hunnewell and went into camp, followed closely by the troops. At Hunnewell the cavalry camped on one side of the creek and the colonists on the other. During the three days they were there, awaiting a reply to their petition to Washington, they were joined by scores of new recruits who had been literally starved out of the dry regions of western Kansas. Hundreds more from the surrounding area came to stare curiously at the throng.

On Sunday morning, December 12, the colonists paraded through the streets of Hunnewell, 600 strong, with 325 wagons. That afternoon in camp a religious service was conducted by the colony chaplain. The officers and soldiers across the creek were invited, and seats were provided for some forty ladies.

The service opened with singing "America." The text was from Exodus: "The Lord commandeth unto Moses to go forth and possess the promised land!" The next song was:

> "Hold the fort for we are coming,
> Oklahoma still."

The service was closed with a spirited rendition of "The Star-Spangled Banner," three cheers for the flag, three more for the president, and a tiger for the federal troops. The Stars and Stripes displayed about the camp fanned the breeze, while a number of the wagons were adorned with the same colors of Old Glory and banners with such mottoes as "On to Oklahoma," "No Turn Back!" "Strike for Homes!" "Uncle Sam is rich enough to give us all a home in Oklahoma." It was a novel spectacle. The troops were visibly affected.

That night the colony held a council to decide what course to pursue. They voted to wait a day longer. Perhaps there would be some modification of the president's order, and they would be able to proceed.

No answer came from Washington. The colonists' anxiety

Sunday service in boomer camp at Hunnewell, Kansas, December 12, 1880. *From* Frank Leslie's Illustrated Newspaper, *Jan. 1, 1881.*

increased. Some proposed to enter the lands despite the military. Another meeting was held.

Dr. Robert Wilson of Texas was appointed to go to Washington to see what could be done. To relieve the critical situation, the colonists broke camp and moved farther west to Caldwell, and the soldiers followed.

En route to Caldwell the colony was joined by five more wagons and twenty men. The mayor and a large group of citizens came out to welcome the colonists and escorted them through the streets lined with cheering men and women waving handkerchiefs.

The following day the citizens of Caldwell held a mass meeting. They adopted a resolution endorsing the movement and requesting the president to order the troops to accompany the settlers into Oklahoma as an escort.

But Washington officials remained adamant. Unable to influence them through petition, the colonists became restless. To keep them from disbanding, Captain Payne, with a small group, quietly crossed the line into the Oklahoma lands, and on May 2 founded on the banks of the Canadian River the first boomer settlement, which he named "New Philadelphia."

He was immediately arrested by troops from Fort Reno, charged with trespassing on Indian reservations, and his colony driven back to Kansas.

At his trial in the United States District Court at Fort Smith, Arkansas, Payne's attorney, Judge Baker of St. Louis, argued at length the character of the treaty with the Indians in 1866. The court was undecided. Secretary of Interior Carl Schurz held that these lands had been obtained exclusively for the use of freedmen or Indians who would accept the civilizing influences of the nation. But the ablest lawyers of the country disagreed, holding with Payne that they were public domain and, therefore, subject to pre-emption and settlement.

Payne was released on bond, and following his later attempts to settle in the territory from 1881 to 1883, the performance was repeated—the boomers were arrested, their property was destroyed, and they were forced to return to Kansas and released, Payne each time demanding a trial before the courts and not getting it.

His failures made him a martyr. He founded his own newspaper, the Oklahoma *War Chief,* to combat adverse publicity. He stirred up so much sentiment that in most of the important cities of Texas, Arkansas, and Kansas colonies were formed in favor of the movement.

Originally there had been two boomer organizations formed in the winter of 1879–80, with headquarters in Wichita. The first was Payne's Oklahoma Colony, with Payne as president. The other was the Oklahoma Town Company, later the Southwestern Colonization Society, composed largely of Wichita businessmen who took no part in the invasions.

Because of growing Wichita opposition as to how his campaign was being conducted, Payne, in March, 1883, moved his headquarters to Geuda Springs, between Caldwell and Arkansas City. Wichita officials thought he should concentrate on opening the Oklahoma lands. Payne now included the Cherokee Outlet.

Under the treaties with the Cherokees, Creeks, Seminoles, Choctaws, and Chickasaws, the western boundaries of their lands had not been accurately defined. The outlets were hunting highways, varying from fourteen to one hundred miles wide, extending to the Rocky Mountains and reserved to the Indians for buffalo hunting. With the buffalo gone and the Plains tribes now occupying most of the western half of the Territory, the purpose of these outlets no longer existed. Therefore, claimed Payne, the whole domain actually was a part of the public land and subject to settlement.

His appeals attracted men in high position. Doctors, judges, railroad officials, and big daily newspapers such as the Chicago *Times,* Kansas City *Times,* and Topeka *Commonwealth* purchased colony shares. On a speaking tour that took him as far east as St. Louis and Springfield, in January, 1884, he drew enthusiastic crowds, and thousands joined the movement in Iowa, Illinois, Ohio, Kentucky, Indiana, and New York.

In February and March Payne carried his fight to Washington. In executive offices, crowded hotels, and on the streets he told how he had been "hunted down" by vindictive civil and military forces of the federal government, and variously dubbed the "notorious captain," the "border dead beat," and "Oklahoma outlaw," when his only crime was seeking a home for himself and his people upon public domain.

Fearlessly he charged that the Cherokee Livestock Association, with headquarters at Caldwell, had so bribed and sold shares of stock to army officers, members of Congress, and other government officials, that it held the army, legislature, and courts at its bidding. A committee was appointed to investigate, but nothing came of it.

His funds exhausted, Payne returned to Kansas. Immediately he began preparations for a new invasion of the Indian Territory. He announced that the boomers would start for the "promised land" on June 25, and celebrate the Fourth of July with a barbecue on the banks of the North Canadian. But Payne took suddenly ill, and the planned invasion was called off.

Payne and his boomers stopping to bridge Deep Fork on the
Canadian in 1883.

The boomers celebrated the Fourth of July at Geuda Springs. Payne rose from his sickbed to assure them that soon the government would no longer be able to keep them out and all who joined him would be rewarded with the richest lands on the American continent.

Forthwith he moved 1,500 boomers to the north bank of the Chikaskia, five miles south of Hunnewell, in the Cherokee Outlet. They set up tents, built dugouts, and erected a frame building for the *War Chief*.

On August 7 soldiers surrounded the camp. They seized the *War Chief* and burned the office. J. B. Cooper, the editor; Captain Payne and his lieutenant, William L. Couch; Couch's two sons, and the colony surveyor were arrested without the formality of warrants, and the rest of the boomers marched back to Kansas. The prisoners were placed in irons and again taken three hundred miles to Fort Smith and discharged without trial.

Back in Kansas, Payne and the others voluntarily appeared before a federal grand jury at Wichita. Determined to test the legality of their cause, they gave evidence of their invasion of Oklahoma, and were indicted for conspiracy against the government. Their attorney, J. Wade McDonald, so ably presented the case before federal Judge C. G. Foster that the latter decided that trespass on Oklahoma lands did not show a conspiracy to commit an offense against the United States within the meaning of the statute, and he quashed the indictments.

Payne's colony met at Arkansas City on November 20, and proposed again to invade Oklahoma as soon as Judge Foster's decision reached Washington and new orders reached the military in the Indian Territory.

At Wellington, on November 26, Captain Payne delivered

Payne's last boomer camp in the unassigned lands, in 1883.

to a large crowd of boomers and citizens one of the finest speeches of his career. He retired to his room in the Hotel DeBarnard. The next morning he entered the dining room with his friends. He ate a hearty breakfast, then ordered a glass of milk. While waiting, he suddenly slumped forward in his chair.

His friends sprang to his side, unbuttoned his collar, and started rubbing his wrists vigorously. But it was no use. His body grew tense, the muscles in his neck stood out like whip-cords. A moment later he was dead.

Thousands came to pay their respects and attend the last rites in Woodlawn Cemetery, and his buoyant spirit rebounded to give new impetus to the movement.

At a mass meeting of the Oklahoma Colony, William L. Couch, Payne's faithful aid and most trusted friend and adviser, was elected president and captain.

Couch was born in North Carolina, the eldest of seven children. At the outbreak of the Civil War his father, M. H. Couch, had decided to join the Union army, and young William carried provisions to him at night in a cave, where he hid, waiting an opportunity to slip through Confederate lines to Louisville, Kentucky. M. H. Couch was rejected by the Union army because of a speech impediment, and he moved his family to Kansas.

During the war Confederate soldiers plundered the Couch home. In 1867 the family moved to Johnson County, Kansas, where young William grew up. At twenty-one he owned his farm, and later operated farms in Sedgwick and Sumner counties. From 1876 to 1884 he dealt in horses and cattle, and was only thirty-four when elected head of the Oklahoma Colony.

Captain William L. Couch.

An intelligent, persistent man, he knew all the treaties, laws, and court decisions affecting the Oklahoma lands. While he respected the judgment of the President of the United States, he reserved the right to disagree with him, and questioned the authority of the military to tie and drag persons behind wagons in removing them from Indian Territory.

Seven troops of the Ninth Cavalry had been in Indian Territory guarding the Oklahoma lands at the time of Payne's arrest at Rock Falls in 1884. With Payne's death and apparent disbanding of the boomers, five troops were ordered back to their proper stations. Only Troops I and L were kept in the field during the winter. Troop L was stationed at Caldwell, Kansas. Troop I, a unit of forty men under the command of Lieutenant M. W. Day, was stationed at a place twenty miles southwest of present Stillwater known as Camp Russell.

Captain Couch lost no time in asserting the boomers' claims. On December 8, 1884, he left the Kansas line at the head of 164 armed men, bound for the unassigned lands. They followed the old "Payne Trail" from Arkansas City via the Ponca Agency and Red Rock in the Otoe reservation, and four days later had set up winter headquaters in a horseshoe bend of Stillwater Creek a half mile above its junction with the Boomer.

Forty-two strong dugouts were built in a hill in the bend of the creek, both for protection from the cold north wind and as fortifications. There was an abundance of game, timber, water, good drainage, and a suitable place to ford the stream. The site was only sixty-five miles south of Arkansas City, not too far from reinforcements and supplies, and a member made frequent trips to the Pawnee Agency on horseback and brought mail to the camp.

A town company of eighty men was organized. They platted a townsite and selected claims along Stillwater Creek. The day before Christmas the weather was exceedingly cold and all the streams were frozen. The colonists were busily engaged in the construction of several cabins when one of their hunters brought word that a cavalry unit of forty soldiers and two six-mule teams were approaching the camp.

Everyone was called from his work. Quickly they massed in a line, four and five deep, armed with double-barreled shotguns and rifles. Lieutenant Day and his soldiers moved up. He placed thirty men on a skirmish line and ordered Couch to submit to arrest and the colonists to lay down their arms and surrender. This they refused to do, and Couch asked Day for his authority.

Day replied: "I have only one authority, the carbine."

"That is an authority we do not recognize," replied Couch.

Couch was standing about thirty feet in advance of the hastily assembled colonists. Lieutenant Day ordered eight men to tie him. As the soldiers advanced to execute the order, Couch levered a cartridge into the barrel of his Winchester.

"If you lay a hand on me," he said, "I will consider it an assault and treat it as such."

Lieutenant Day ordered his men back to the skirmish line and commanded them to load. Then he told the colonists they had five minutes to surrender or he would open fire.

The colonists didn't surrender, nor did the troops open fire. They were so densely massed that Day hesitated to give the command "as the slaughter would have been great." Too, he knew several of the boomers, having met them in the Indian Territory on previous occasions, and still believed they would lay down their arms. He called them insurgents for not submitting to arrest, and still holding his watch in his hand, he extended the time five minutes.

The colonists had been standing where the bank of the creek rose as a terrace, before their dugouts and tents and wagons. They now fled into the dugouts and behind wagons and trees, determined to resist, leaving Day no alternative but "to lay siege to the place and treat them as Indians."

To arrest them without bloodshed called for reinforcements. In that ten minutes he had counted 225 men, a few boys, and one woman. He was outnumbered twenty to one. He wanted to do his duty in every way, but he could not bluff them and was too weak to fight them. Finally he asked Couch:

"Well, Captain, where is a good place to camp? My men are freezing here."

Couch replied: "Camp down the creek; we will be neighborly."

Day pitched camp about eighty rods from the boomers and sent a courier for reinforcements. In his message to the post adjutant at Fort Reno he made the first official mention of the name of the new town when he wrote: "The settlers call this place Stillwater."

Captain Couch also sent a courier to Arkansas City, and from there sent a telegram to President Chester A. Arthur stating that it was unnecessary to send more troops against the boomers; that if he would send one United States marshal with a legal warrant and promise them a trial in any court, everyone would submit to arrest.

The boomers considered themselves under the jurisdiction of civil law, and did not intend again to be "dragged to Fort Reno and from there to some state line to be turned loose without recourse of law" by the military. Couch asked if the president would "assume the responsibility" of declaring them insurgent citizens of the United States for locating upon and occupying public domain.

On Christmas Day the weather turned wet and colder. Lieutenant Day and his troops remained in camp and sent one wagon back to Camp Russell for rations. From December 26 to 29 it rained and sleeted. Out in the storm, without tents, several of the soldiers were on sick report with frost-bites, and one threatened with pneumonia. The doctor at Stillwater gave him some medicine, and he was sent back to Camp Russell. Day reported: "He is better now." At noon on the twenty-ninth, Day received an order by courier from Major Thomas B. Dewees, commanding the Ninth Cavalry at Fort Reno, to return to Camp Russell and await reinforcements. At the same time Dewees urged headquarters to send at least two additional troops to Camp Russell.

That evening a heavy norther blew in with snow. The storm increased during the night. At eight o'clock the next morning the troops broke camp. Day left Sergeant Wilson and four men at Stillwater with rations and forage for ten days. Sergeant Wilson was to send him a courier every day to report plans, arrivals, and departures of the intruders.

Day was confident the boomers would not move farther into Oklahoma as they wanted to settle the Oklahoma question at once and forever. To do this, they must keep their forces together, and Stillwater was more easily supplied than any point south of the Cimarron. The country was a glare of ice. It was impossible for even the cavalry to march more than fifteen miles per day.

Despite these conditions, more wagons and boomers were arriving almost every hour. Seven wagons and seventeen colonists came in at Stillwater the day the troops left, and

the leaders were sending for their friends with the promise
that the troops would not be allowed to arrest them.

"No danger to Sergeant Wilson and his party is to be
apprehended," Day reported to Fort Reno. The boomers had
become "exceedingly friendly" and had "stopped carrying
their arms in their hands." They had even loaned Day a
spring wagon and team to come out and meet the supply
wagon and carry rations to Sergeant Wilson and the four men
who remained at Stillwater.

This fraternizing of the soldiers and settlers didn't set well
with Lieutenant General Philip H. Sheridan, commanding
the Department of the Missouri. In a telegram which Richard
C. Drum, adjutant general of the Army, sent to General
C. C. Augur at Fort Leavenworth, Sheridan thought Lieutenant Day "entirely too familiar with the intruders; that he
should be cautioned in this respect and informed that the
performance of duty should not be embarrassed by exhibition of sympathy. . . ." Thus Lieutenant Day passed from
Oklahoma history and efforts to remove the boomers fell into
the hands of officers of higher rank.

In compliance with Special Orders, Department of the
Missouri, Colonel Edward Hatch of the Ninth Cavalry arrived at Troop L headquarters in Caldwell on December 30.
A native of Maine, he had been a Union soldier under
General Grant in the South, commanding the entire cavalry
division in the Army of the Tennessee. He was made briga-
dier general in 1864. His gallantry in the field caused his
further promotion to the rank of brevet major general and
his transfer from the volunteer to the regular army as colonel
of the Ninth Cavalry. He had succeeded General Gordon
Grander as commander of the Department of Arizona, which
included New Mexico, in 1876; negotiated a treaty with the

Ute Indians in 1880; and was widely known as an Indian fighter when he arrived at Caldwell. Hatch immediately put Troop L in condition for winter field service and had the horses shod for winter travel.

Hatch seemed to have a better understanding of the Oklahoma situation than most military men on the frontier. While preparing for the expedition to Camp Russell and Stillwater, and waiting to be reinforced with two troops from Fort Riley, he reported to his superiors that the settlers were in the Oklahoma lands on advice of their leaders and lawyers that they had a right to resist by arms any attempt to remove them. One had only to look at the newspapers of the surrounding states to realize the sentiment by which these people were actuated, Hatch said. There were at least ten other colonies already organized for an invasion of the country, and although he felt his present force sufficient to expel the armed intruders at Stillwater, it would be entirely insufficient to resist the hordes of not less than 20,000 that would swarm in from Kansas, Missouri, and Arkansas in the spring.

On January 7, the day Hatch and his detachment left Caldwell, he wrote a letter urging Congress either to declare the Oklahoma lands open to settlement, or pass laws providing penalties for invasion of Indian Territory and confiscation of buildings; that unless this was done, the government would be compelled, at great expense, to keep a force in the Oklahoma country large enough to guard every thoroughfare, river, and watercourse.

"The impression that legislation now before the House of Congress will extinguish at an early day the leases by cattlemen on the Cherokee Strip adds largely to the embarrassment in protecting these lands. The cattle proprietors, in sustaining their leases from the Indians, numbering with their

Senator Preston B. Plumb of Kansas who supported the
boomers' invasion of Oklahoma lands. *Courtesy Kansas State
Historical Society.*

employees some thousands of determined men, have so far been an important element in holding Indian lands from settlement. . . . It requires little discernment to foresee that it will not be a great while before the resistance must lead to serious loss of life. . . ."

Two days later Senator Preston B. Plumb, of Kansas, presented to the Senate a memorial addressed to Congress signed by 154 names of "the people of Oklahoma, assembled in public meeting, at the town of Stillwater" requesting immediate attention to the following facts:

"Oklahoma was bought by the United States from the Creek and Seminole Indians eighteen years ago. It has been paid for in full. The title rests solely and exclusively in the United States. There are no limitations of any kind whatever. No Indian or tribe of Indians owns, or claims to own, controls, or claims to control, one foot of these lands.

". . . We thoroughly and with one accord believe that our right to make homes for ourselves and our families upon these lands would not have been questioned had it not been that the rich cattle syndicates were here ahead of us.

"These men are few in number, but strong in the use of unlimited capital.

"They do not pretend to have even a lease of these lands from any source whatever, yet they hold and enclose them with wire fences, and the federal army is used as their private police.

"We are here with our axes and our plows. Hundreds and thousands of our friends are on their way to join us from all the states of the West.

"We are here to stay. We deny the right of any man, or mob of men, whether in uniform or plain clothes, to molest us. . . ."

Senator Plumb did not agree on the title to the Oklahoma lands. The United States had purchased only the right to use them for location of Indians and freedmen. Title to the lands remained with the Creeks and Seminoles. Cattlemen, not Indians and freedmen, were using them, but the government considered their occupancy as temporary and transitory. Homesteading was a different matter.

Senator Plumb admitted that while the settlers at Stillwater were there "technically at least in violation of the law, or at all events in violation of the law as construed by the attorney general and as understood by the president," at the same time the violation was "merely technical," and he urged that Congress take action at once.

Meanwhile, the rain, snow, and cold weather were hampering the progress of Colonel Hatch and his troops on their march to the south. The troops arrived at the Arkansas River on January 15. For twenty-four hours reliefs of men worked steadily with buckets, camp kettles, and cooking utensils, throwing water on the crossing selected, until a sufficient thickness of ice was formed to carry the command across safely.

As Hatch resumed his march south from the Arkansas, Captain Francis Moore, with three troops, was ordered to proceed to Stillwater Creek, take up positions north and east, cut off all supplies and reinforcements proceeding to the colony, and await the arrival of the troops from Fort Reno and Camp Russell.

When Hatch reached Camp Russell and read Sergeant Wilson's reports, he sent this dispatch to headquarters: "Strength of boomers increasing. Count by sergeant on 15th, 375. No question they will fight."

General Augur at Fort Leavenworth wired the adjutant

general: "Should he [Hatch] be right, and they fire upon the troops, it is understood they are to be treated as public enemies, and to be captured or killed. . . . Answer as soon as convenient. Have put all troops at Reno under Hatch's orders."

Troop I was moved from Camp Russell to near Stillwater to intercept parties and supplies. Troops at Fort Reno under Major Dewees, delayed by a severe snowstorm, started for the boomer colony January 18. On January 19 the number of settlers at Stillwater had increased to 400. On January 20 Adjutant General Drum sent Augur a telegram containing instructions from Lieutenant General Sheridan: "The president's order for the removal from the Indian Territory of the intruders therein is to be enforced. It is hoped that it may be done without an armed conflict; but the responsibility for any bloodshed must rest upon those who do not accept the warning.

"You will immediately reinforce Colonel Hatch by the remaining companies of the Ninth Cavalry, and also send him reinforcements from the tenth, twentieth, and twenty-second regiments of infantry, until the force he now has in hand shall be increased by eight hundred. . . ."

Augur transmitted the telegram to Hatch, and added: "Read this to the intruders and direct their surrender. If they refuse, you need not proceed to extremities until your reinforcements arrive, but cut off all supplies possible and prevent others from joining them. . . . Should any of the intruders desire to come in, you should receive them and send them out of the country, except such as are recognized as the leaders. These are to be held until they can be turned over to civil authority."

Accordingly, Hatch had Sergeant Wilson circulate through

the colony a paper which stated in part: "It is within the knowledge of the officer in command that some hundreds of men have banded together to resist with arms the execution of the law in avowed insurrection against the government. . . . It must be clearly understood that the killing of any soldier obeying orders in the execution of his duty by men armed to resist the law is simply murder, and that they will sooner or later be tried for the same as principals or accessories. . . . Legislation is open to settle any grievance; there is no necessity to resort to arms. All trouble can easily be avoided by observing the proclamation of the President of the United States and peaceably leaving the territory as directed. . . ."

To which Couch replied: "I claim the right to defend myself against any person who is not backed with a legal process. . . . I deny that the military process is legal. . . . I consider that the courts are the proper places to settle a point of law. We have endeavored to get a decision and we have been trifled with by both the Army and the courts. . . .

"We are not in rebellion against our country. We have raised no insurrection, and it must be distinctly understood that if a drop of blood is spilled, it will be at your hands.

"You should also remember that 'no one is so exalted as to be above the law,' not even the President of the United States. . . .

"We agree that there need be no difficulty, and if you observe the law as closely as we do, there will be none."

Sergeant Wilson informed Hatch that Couch and his party were throwing up rifle pits in the frozen ground. Major Dewees reached Camp Russell with Troops G and C of the Ninth and Company D of the Twentieth Infantry, which were moved to Stillwater Creek at once.

Certain that he was unknown to the boomers, and "desirous of knowing their condition for resistance," Hatch rode over to the settlement alone on January 23. The rifle pits were large enough to contain fifty men. The dugouts were so arranged to be "capable of being used for this purpose also."

On the evening of the twenty-fourth, Hatch's command moved to within four hundred yards of the colony. Excluding the force left at Camp Russell, and the detachments watching the trails and patrolling, he had more than three hundred men ready for action.

The proximity of the troops increased tension in the colony. The quick-tempered faction of the boomers wanted to open fire on the soldiers and get it over with as soon as possible, and it was all Couch could do to convince them that they should not fire unless fired upon.

In a final effort to obtain their surrender, Lieutenant F. W. Finley visited the colony and read them the instructions of the General of the Army.

Couch replied: "We had that from the newspapers some two days ago. We do not intend to leave, neither will we do so as long as we can resist with arms."

What happened afterward is put down in Hatch's report as follows: "The 25th was spent in working upon the fears of the timid. . . . One of the citizen teamsters learned there were but two days' rations in the Boomer camp, and that they were anxiously looking for one hundred men from Kansas by way of Hunnewell. . . . It was also discovered during the night there was dissension among the leaders as to the best course to pursue. We promptly decided to move boldly upon them in the morning, trusting the result would be favorable. The usual orders were issued for going into action, care being observed that the order should reach their camp that night. This with a note by a friendly party to the only woman begging her to leave early in the morning.

"In the morning the command formed for moving. The company of Infantry to seize a hill covering the rifle pits and defensible dugouts. Major Dewees with four troops dismounted to move directly upon the headquarters and the leaders.

"Captain Moore, with three troops dismounted on Dewees' left, and should we be compelled to fight to take their camp in reverse. I then with my adjutant rode into their camp, telling them as much as we regretted bloodshed, we should open fire at the first effort at armed resistance. Couch at first refused to go, then asked for time which was declined. Finding the troops would be upon him in a moment more, gave up further opposition, and would do as directed. It was apparent he had his followers under reasonable control. It then became a question as to the best means of removing them to the Kansas border; should they be placed under guard, it devolved upon us to ration them and forage their animals. It was known to me the leaders were abundantly supplied with money, and in a day's march we could reach the Pawnees, where rations and forage could be obtained.

"Couch was then informed he should keep his men together, arms packed in wagons and all effects should be transported by them, that they should furnish their rations and forage and be marched out to the Kansas line, subject to being at any time placed in the hands of the U. S. Marshal, all parties out to be called in, and any wagons that he was aware of coming into the country, which might escape the troops, to be turned back by him. In doing this I was enabled to send Major Dewees to the south side of the Cimarron, and dispatch a force toward the Arkansas River, to prevent the arrival of a large number of intruders who were reported coming from Arkansas by way of the Sac and Fox agency, and also to send a troop to look after and intercept the men from Hunnewell. It would have been more satisfactory to have taken them out under close guard, under the circumstances, believe the other was the best action to be taken, camping with them until their last night when I rode to Hunnewell, having the proper warrants served by the U. S. Marshal on the leaders, with arrest for unlawfully entering on Indian lands with the view of permanent occupancy."

In a speech which he delivered before the Oklahoma Convention at Topeka, Kansas, February 3, Captain Couch gave this version: "An order was sent us Sunday, January 25, to surrender. We again refused, but declined to fight only in self-defense. Sunday night we received another order, which was likewise refused. Monday morning the military forces under Hatch were formed in line with two pieces of artillery. The colonel rode over and asked us what we proposed to do. We told him that as long as we were free American citizens, we would not submit to being harassed by the military, since we were committing no crime. We found our rations would last but five days and we could not make a stand, so we concluded to vacate in two days, but not in obedience to any time set by Hatch, and we moved out without escort.

"At Arkansas City we were met by an immense concourse of people with a brass band. Our colors were flying during our trip and during our stay—an evidence of our loyalty to the United States government."

In his letter to the adjutant general, Department of Missouri, on January 30, Hatch admitted: "Had the troops with me arrived a few days later, the settlement of the matter might have been delayed. They came up in time to prevent junction of reinforcements from different points and arrival of supplies to provision them [the boomers] for a month."

He reported that the leaders were being held for a hearing on February 10, but that "such is the sentiment of southern Kansas on this question, it will be questionable whether a conviction can be obtained."

Couch and the others were never tried, and they planned another invasion of the Oklahoma lands for March 4. But public opinion had swung in their favor, and they were persuaded to quit raiding the unassigned lands and start raiding the President and Congress.

As a result, the Secretary of the Interior negotiated a settlement with the Creeks and Seminoles, in which they relinquished all claims to the Oklahoma district for four million dollars. A rider was attached to the congressional enactment providing that any person who entered the region prior to its lawful opening would forfeit all rights to a homestead. An appropriation bill containing the agreement also authorized the President to open the lands under the terms of the homestead law.

On April 22, 1889, what is now central Oklahoma was opened by a "run" in which fifty thousand homeseekers took claims. On that day an embryo state was founded, with six counties, one of which was named "Payne" in honor of Captain David L. Payne, the Father of Oklahoma.

Captain Couch made the run and staked a claim at the west edge of Oklahoma City. He was elected the town's first mayor and served with honor until April 14, 1890, when he was shot and killed by J. C. Adams, a trespasser. He was buried at Oklahoma City in Fairlawn Cemetery.

Like Captain Payne, he gave the best years of his life for something he never lived to enjoy.

10. Amos Chapman

Buckskin Hero

IN exploring the Western wilderness and guarding the frontiers, the army found constant need of men experienced in the craft of the plains and with a knowledge of Indian language and habits. Of all frontiersmen, trappers made the best scouts and guides. They had learned their lessons from the Indians; they knew every landmark, water hole, the nature of the soil.

Although an army officer, with his instruments and general knowledge of the country, could take a command safely through an unknown region, it could be done with much less delay and suffering by using the services of a scout.

Many scouts' names will never be forgotten—Jim Bridger, Kit Carson, Frémont's famous scouts; California Joe, made immortal by General George A. Custer, and Wild Bill and Buffalo Bill employed by Custer, Merritt, and Carr. The story of their lives is the history of the West.

The success of every expedition depended not only on their skill and intelligence in providing good routes and comfortable camps, but they were relied upon for knowledge of the position and movements of the enemy.

This information could be gained only by scouting far in advance, or out from the flanks of the columns. And this often tested a valuable quality that not all of them possessed—courage.

Strangely, these frontiersmen, so utterly adept at shooting each other for pastime, were sometimes less courageous when facing Indians. Even Kit Carson, "the bravest of the brave," would not fight if he could avoid it.

As Colonel Richard I. Dodge wrote:

Of ten men employed as scouts, nine will be worthless. Of fifty so employed, one may prove to be really valuable. . . . Though hundreds, even thousands of men have been so employed by the government . . . the number of really remarkable men among them can be counted on the fingers.

One of these, says Dodge, was Amos Chapman.

History does not record the date of his birth. He was said to have been eighty-four when he died July 18, 1925, on his ranch four miles east of Seiling, Oklahoma. He had spent his life there with his Indian family and relatives after retiring from government service.

It is unfortunate that someone did not take the trouble to record the desperate adventures and hairbreadth escapes he experienced in his fifteen years with the army. No doubt they would have filled volumes. But the feat which proved his courage, and for which Congress awarded him the Medal of Honor, occurred in the fight at Buffalo Wallow, just west of

Amos Chapman's historic rescue of his comrade in the Battle of Buffalo Wallow. *From* Our Wild Indians, *1882, by Richard I. Dodge.*

Colonel Richard I. Dodge who said: "Of hundreds, even thousands, of men employed by the government as scouts, the number of really remarkable ones can be counted on the fingers." One of these was Amos Chapman. *From* Our Wild Indians, *1882, by Richard I. Dodge.*

the Oklahoma-Texas panhandle boundary on September 12, 1874.

The Medicine Lodge Treaty had been signed only a few years before. The government had agreed to its terms that buffalo hunters would never cross south of the Arkansas River. But Texas, when admitted to the Union, had reserved all public land. Not having been consulted in the treaty, the state made no effort to prevent the invasion of hunters within its borders.

The result was that the combined tribes of the Southwest were on the warpath. Chaos reigned; murder swept the land.

General Nelson A. Miles was commanding the expedition against the wild tribes of the Indian Territory, with Camp Supply as his base of operations. In September, 1874, he was camped on McClellan Creek awaiting reinforcements and supplies before proceeding against the marauders to force them to surrender or participate in a decisive battle.

The Indians had retreated to the fastness of the canyon country of the Texas panhandle. In their flight they had cut behind him and intercepted his trains, leaving him without sufficient food and ammunition. When General Miles realized his supplies were low, and that he probably had been out-witted by the enemy, he detailed Scouts Chapman and Billy Dixon to inform department headquarters at Camp Supply of the seriousness of the situation.

He offered them as many soldier escorts as they deemed necessary. They reasoned that secrecy would be more dependable than large but insufficient numbers, and chose to take only four men—Sergeant L. T. Woodhall and Privates Peter Rath, John Harrington, and George Smith.

The six men traveled for two nights, concealing themselves during daylight. On the morning of September 12, while searching for a place of concealment, they topped a rise and found themselves surrounded by a hundred and twenty-five Kiowa and Comanche warriors.

Realizing that whatever chance they had lay in making a standing fight together, they dismounted. The Indians charged them, yelling and firing their weapons. The scout party drove the Indians back, but in this first attack every man of the six was wounded, Smith fatally. Their horses stampeded with coats, canteens, and haversacks attached to the saddles.

Without food or water, and in a badly exposed position, the situation seemed hopeless. Then the keen eyes of Chapman spotted a buffalo wallow a hundred yards away. It was a slight depression on the prairie, only ten feet in diameter.

One after the other, all the men except Smith, reached it. While the soldiers kept firing, Chapman and Dixon worked with bowie knives to deepen the depression and throw soil around the rim for additional protection.

Under almost constant fire, outnumbered twenty-five to one, the little party of five defended their lives. Down the slope Smith lay where he had fallen, presumably dead. When the excitement of the first charge of the Indians had quieted down, the supposedly dead man began to move.

Immediately the Indians began firing at him. To leave him out there, helpless to reach the shelter under his own power, meant certain death.

Chapman told his comrades:

"Keep them off me! I'm going down to get Smith."

As the hostiles charged, the besieged men opened fire. Leaving his rifle behind, Chapman sprang over the rim and ran full speed to Smith. He seized and shouldered him and began staggering under his weight back to the shelter. Thirty

yards away a dozen Indians swooped down at him on running ponies.

The Indians recognized him and yelled in their own
tongue:

"Amos! Amos! We have got you now!"

Chapman drew his pistol. Unable to hold Smith on his
back with one hand, he let the trooper fall. From the buffalo
wallow his companions fired a fusillade, and Chapman began
firing his pistol.

The Indians scattered, yelling and tumbling from their
ponies, dead. A few escaped. The way was clear, and Chapman again lifted Smith to his shoulder in an effort to reach
the wallow.

His pistol was empty, and this time he did not stop to fight.
Twenty yards from the wallow a gaudily painted savage rode
almost upon him and fired. Chapman felt his left leg collapse,
and he fell with Smith on top of him.

Again his comrades opened fire, and the Indians withdrew,
losing most of their number in the charge. Chapman jumped
up, picked up Smith, and this time gained the safety of the
wallow.

"Amos," exclaimed Dixon, "you're badly wounded!"

"Naw," Chapman replied.

"Look at your leg," said Dixon.

Glancing at his leg, Chapman saw that it had been shot
off above the ankle. In his last desperate effort to save the
life of a comrade he had walked on bone, dragging his foot
behind him.

Smith had been shot through a lung. When he breathed,
the air sobbed from beneath his shoulder blade. Dixon got a
willow stock that one of the charging Indians had been using

for a quirt and stuffed a silk handkerchief into the wound to stop the bleeding.

With Smith sitting upright in the wallow, the others moving with brave and painful effort to conceal their crippled condition, they fought the Indians until dark, sometimes at such short range that they used their pistols, retaining the last charge to prevent capture and torture.

Discouraged in their efforts to best the white men, the prairie strewn with their dead, the Indians made no further attack. A cold rain began to fall, and the whole band disappeared.

That night Private Smith died. The wounded survivors lay in the wallow and drank the rain water that collected in a pool mingled with their own blood while Dixon rode for help.

At Camp Supply the surgeon amputated Chapman's leg below the knee. A week later he had to hide the scout's clothing to keep him in bed.

"He remained in government employ for years afterward," Colonel Dodge related, "as useful and as ready for a fight as any two-legged scout."

11. Deaf Smith

Fighting Texan

THE Texas revolution had ended. The constitution had designated Austin the permanent capital, where the public archives were kept, reserving for the president the power to order their removal in case of danger from sudden insurrection or attack by a foreign enemy.

A Mexican army had occupied San Antonio. The plains Indians, raiding throughout West Texas, had committed ravages within sight of the capital itself. Sam Houston, deciding that the exceptional emergency had arrived, dispatched an order to his subordinates to send the state records to the temporary seat of government at Washington on the Brazos, and the stormy reaction of the citizens of Austin threatened bloodshed and even civil war.

Hotel and boardinghouse keepers, grocers, gamblers—all read into the measure a deathblow to their businesses, fearing that the removal of the records would mean the final abandonment of the city as the capital.

A mass meeting of citizens and farmers in all the surrounding country was called. Fiery speeches were made against "the asserted tyranny of the administration," and it was unanimously agreed to oppose the execution of Houston's mandate, even to the point of open and armed resistance. A company of four hundred men was organized to guard the state house. Colonel Morton was chosen to command the force.

Morton had achieved considerable notoriety in the War for Independence. More recently he had displayed his bravery in two private encounters in which he had almost cut his antagonists to pieces with a bowie knife. With Morton heading the opposition, it was believed that President Sam Houston would desist in his purpose.

Morton's vanity equaled his prowess. Encouraged by public opinion, he boasted that should an overpowering force march to seize the records for Houston, he personally would "hunt him down" and kill him "with as little ceremony" as he would a wolf. Or he would "stab him in bed," or "waylay him in his walks of recreation." He even sent a message to this effect to the hero of San Jacinto.

Houston laconically replied, "If the people of Austin do not send the archives, I shall certainly take them, and if Colonel Morton can kill me, he is welcome to my ear cap."

Morton ordered sentinels on every road entering the city and had the guard doubled around the state house. Troops paraded the streets day and night. A special caucus went into permanent session at the city hall as the whole town waited for the invasion.

One afternoon the caucus was surprised when a stranger, who, unseen, had climbed a bushy-topped oak outside the wall, without warning leaped through a high window into their chambers.

His appearance was as startling as his entry. He was clad in buckskin from head to foot, carried a long, heavy rifle in his hand and a bowie on a leathern belt, which also supported a pair of pistols nearly half the length of his gun.

He was tall, straight, and moved like a panther. Jet-black hair flowed to his shoulders. His dark face was ironlike, almost severe, and his eyes, a vivid black, were piercing as dagger points, wild and rolling. Every man in the room involuntarily reached for his sidearms.

Colonel Morton stamped toward him. "Who are you, to burst in upon gentlemen without being invited?" he demanded, ferociously trying to stare the stranger down.

The uninvited visitor returned the stare with a cold, sneering gaze, but did not reply, instead, placing a long, bony finger across his lips as if for silence.

"Speak up, or I'll cut an answer from your heart!" shouted Morton.

The stranger's hand dropped from his mouth to the hilt of his huge knife. The enraged colonel whipped out his own blade, but the men restrained him.

"Let him go, Morton!" they pleaded. "Can't you see he's crazy?"

In that crisis Judge Webb, a shrewd, quiet man, stepped forward and spoke to the stranger more respectfully.

"My friend," he said suavely, "I believe you have made a mistake. This is a private meeting."

The stranger did not seem to understand. But he was impressed by the judge's mild, courteous manner, and his rigid face relaxed. Moving suddenly to a table in the center of the room, he seized a pen and scratched across a paper the words: "I am deaf." Then he held it up for all to see, as if in apology for his impoliteness.

Judge Webb took the paper and wrote: "Will you oblige us by explaining your presence at this meeting?"

The stranger produced a letter addressed "To the citizens of Austin."

Judge Webb broke the seal, and all read:

Fellow Citizens—Though in error, and deceived by the arts of traitors, I will give you three days more to decide whether you will surrender the public archives. At the end of that time you will please let me know your decision.

Sam Houston.

The strange messenger waited a few moments, as if for an answer, then turned to leave. But Colonel Morton motioned him back to the table.

Morton wrote: "You were brave enough to insult me with your looks ten minutes ago. Are you brave enough now to give me satisfaction?"

The stranger traced his reply: "At your service!"

Morton wrote again: "Who will be your second?"

The stranger answered in writing: "I seek no advantage and fear none on the part of others. I need no second."

Morton penned: "Name your terms."

Without hesitation the stranger wrote: "Time, sunset this. evening; place, the left bank of the Colorado opposite Austin; weapons, rifles; distance, a hundred yards. Do not fail to be on time!"

Then he took two steps across the floor and disappeared through the window as silently as he had entered.

The men crowded around Morton. "Colonel," exclaimed Judge Webb, "you don't intend to fight that man? He's a

mute, possibly a maniac. Such a meeting will do your reputation no good."

"You are right," agreed Morton, smiling. "Except this mute
happens to be the hero of a dozen battles and at least half as
many bloody duels. He is the favorite emissary and bosom
friend of Houston. If I kill him, I think the president will
give us no further trouble."

"You know this man?" chimed a score of voices together.
"Who is he?"

"Deaf Smith," Morton answered coolly.

"He couldn't be," argued Judge Webb. "Deaf Smith was
slain at San Jacinto."

"That is the story of Smith's death made up by Houston
to save him from the vengeance of Texans on whom he had
spied," said Morton. "I've known the truth over a year."

"Then you are mad yourself!" said Webb. "Deaf Smith has
never missed his mark. He has brought down ravens in their
fastest flight, and killed Mexicans and Comanches at two
hundred and fifty yards."

The reputation of this deaf man was one of the most remarkable in the annals of the West. He had been christened
Drastus Smith. Somewhere he had received a good educa-
tion, for he wrote with amazing correctness and facility. But
no one ever knew where he had been born or anything about
his life before he appeared on the Texas frontier.

When the matter was mentioned, he would always lay a
finger across his lips. If pressed for information, his brow
darkened and his black eyes seemed to shoot fire.

What nature had denied him in the way of hearing had
more than been compensated for in those eyes, so quick and
farseeing that he could discover objects miles away on the
horizon where others could see nothing but prairie and sky.

And his sense of smell was so keen that the Rangers declared he could scent an Indian or Mexican farther than a buzzard could detect the odor of a dead carcass. These qualities had fitted him well for being a spy scout, in which capacity he had rendered great service to Houston's army.

"There can be no disgrace in falling before such a shot," declared Colonel Morton defensively. "And if I succeed, I shall achieve greater glory!"

That evening a vast crowd gathered on the banks of the river across from the capital. There was much excitement. Large sums were wagered on the outcome.

When the red sun touched the western hill rims, the antagonists, armed with long rifles, took their position back to back. A white handkerchief was waved. Each walked forward in opposite directions, for fifty steps, whirled, aimed and fired.

The distance was great, and both paused long enough for the crowd to glimpse their faces and note the striking contrast.

Colonel Morton was smiling, but his expression was murderous. Deaf Smith's face was calm, as passionless as if cast of steel. Morton was dressed in the richest cloth, the very embodiment of the "society" of the great cities with all its flattery and fawning and base cunning; Deaf Smith in smoke-tinted leathers, who had made the inanimate things of the earth his friends—the land and waters, the barren rock and tangled brakes of wild, waving cane his home. But in the Texas of those days all men of courage were peers, regardless of dress or condition.

The two rifles roared simultaneously. Colonel Morton staggered and fell wounded. Deaf Smith, standing straight, reloaded his rifle, then suddenly turned and disappeared into the woods.

A few days later General Houston, accompanied by Smith and ten others, rode into Austin and carried away the state papers without opposition. The Mexican and Indian threat subsided, and after a short interval during which the government was conducted at Washington on the Brazos, Austin resumed its life as the capital.

Deaf Smith remained Houston's personal emissary until the Texas president's death. But it was never forgotten how well he had served Texas in her struggle for independence.

His errors rest in oblivion, his virtues are remembered. In the cemetery at Richmond is the Deaf Smith Memorial Monument, erected by the state. Deaf Smith County in West Texas perpetuates his name.

12. Henry Starr

Angel with Spurs

HENRY STARR was the most unusual train-and-bank robbing outlaw ever to run loose in America. He practiced the bandit trade thirty-one years and had as many holdups to his credit as the James-Younger, Dalton-Doolin gangs combined. He was a dead shot, stealthy, cunning, and a natural leader of men. The gangs he recruited were the most daredevil outfits in the Southwest.

Yet he never, during his long career as a bandit, killed a man while committing a holdup. Only once was he ever caught in the act of robbery, and this was after the climax of his career when he had eclipsed anything accomplished by the James-Younger, Dalton-Doolin gangs by robbing two banks in the same town at the same time!

Nonetheless, he was a loyal friend and intelligent. Educated in the schools of the Cherokee Nation, he spent his spare time between robberies reading the classics, and always carried a few of his favorites in his saddlebags.

There was a deep struggle between good and bad in Starr. Three times he vainly tried to reform. He was to know, for a while, how it felt to be respectable. He once produced a motion picture, *A Debtor to the Law,* his testament to the world that crime does not pay, before making his exit in ignoble fashion.

Perhaps he was unfortunate to have been born in the Indian Territory and grow up in the days of "Hanging Judge" Isaac Charles Parker, when there was "no Sunday west of St. Louis—no God west of Fort Smith." This section was called "Robbers' Roost" and "The Land of the Six-shooter," and the Starrs did nothing to better its sinister reputation. The history of the family is a story of blood.

Henry's father was George "Hop" Starr, half-breed Cherokee son of the old Cherokee outlaw, Tom Starr, and brother of Sam Starr, who married Belle, the outlaw queen. The criminal instinct in Henry's nature was a dark heritage from the Starr strain. His mother was half-Irish and a highly respectable woman.

He was born in a log cabin near Fort Gibson, December 2, 1873, and grew up on the ranches of the Cherokee Nation. He was a crack cowboy, five feet nine inches tall, strong and athletic, with straight black hair, dark brown eyes, and handsome with a swarthy complexion. He never used tobacco, coffee, or liquor, and looked like a youth to be trusted.

Then, at the age of seventeen, he was arrested on a charge of introducing whisky to the Indian Territory and taken to Fort Smith, where he pleaded guilty, was fined, and released. The following February, 1892, he was arrested again, for horse stealing, but the case was dismissed. In August he stole two more horses. This time he was released on bond; he failed

Judge Isaac C. Parker, famous as the hanging judge who twice sentenced Henry Starr to the gallows and twice was reversed by the Supreme Court.

to appear for trial, the bond was forfeited, and a reward issued for his capture. Henry now began the series of crimes that graduated him into the class of the James-Youngers, Daltons, and Doolin.

With Ed Newcome, a Delaware half-breed, and Jesse Jackson, a white man, he held up the Missouri Pacific train at Nowata. He robbed the Schufeldt and Son store at Lenapah in October, and in November held up Carter's store at Sequoyah. Detective H. E. Dickey, of the express company, who investigated the Nowata robbery, went to Fort Smith, obtained a warrant for Starr, and, accompanied by Deputy Marshal Floyd Wilson, set out to hunt the youthful bandit.

They picked up his trail south of Lenapah on December 13 and trailed him to the California Creek country near the ranch of Albert Dodge. Dodge told the officers he had seen the outlaw in the area, and the officers began searching for him.

Wilson was alone when he rode up on Starr near Wolf Creek. Sighting each other at the same time, both men dropped from their saddles, with Winchesters in their hands. They faced each other across an opening less than thirty paces apart.

Wilson told Starr he carried a warrant for his arrest and demanded that he surrender, and Starr fired a bullet past Wilson's head to frighten him. Wilson fired back. As he levered for a fresh cartridge, the empty shell jammed in his rifle. Throwing the weapon down, he reached for his revolver. But Starr fired two more shots, and Wilson dropped to the ground. While he lay there, too badly wounded to lift the six-shooter he had drawn, the outlaw calmly strode forward and fired another bullet into his heart, holding the gun so close that the blaze spouting from its muzzle scorched the

The old federal building with its basement jail at Fort Smith, Arkansas, where thousands of prisoners were tried and confined for violations in Oklahoma while Judge Parker reigned from 1875 to 1896. Starr spent five years in jail here pending appeals to the Supreme Court. He read much and wrote articles for newspapers about the Indian Territory and the Five Civilized Tribes.

officer's clothing. The shooting frightened away their horses, but Starr managed to catch Wilson's. He mounted and rode off.

Detective Dickey heard the shooting and hurried to the scene. But he arrived too late. He took Wilson's body back to Fort Smith.

Starr became the most hunted desperado in the Territory. Under his planning and leadership, his fast-shooting, hard-riding band now committed robberies in rapid succession: the railroad station at Chelsea; the Missouri, Kansas, and Texas railroad at Pryor Creek; a railroad station and store at Chouteau; a store at Nowata; the bank at Aldrich, Missouri, and the Caney Valley bank in Kansas.

In the double robbery at Chouteau he met with a couple of disappointments. With two of his gang he rode in to rob the eight-o'clock northbound passenger train, but arrived just as it was leaving the station. They held up the station agent and four passengers who had just got off the train, obtaining $180.

They rode over to Haden's store, where W. A. Hancock, a clerk, was on duty. The store did most of the banking for the cattlemen in the area and usually had five or six thousand dollars in its safe. But Hancock had taken the money to the Vinita bank the day before. Starr cursed him, smashed out the front windows with the stock of his Winchester, and left.

The bank robbery at Aldrich netted the most money, more than $3,000; the Caney holdup was the most daring.

Tying their horses within a block of the bank, Starr and one companion, unmasked and carrying Winchesters, walked boldly into the front door of the bank and covered the officials. The cashier leaped into the vault and slammed the door. When they threatened to kill the president, he opened it and handed over $2,000. The robbers marched their captives into the back yard, which was surrounded by a high board fence, and locked them in. Then calmly they returned to their horses, mounted, and rode into the hills before the people discovered their bank had been looted.

Always on the go, always pursued, they somehow always managed to avoid the marshals until they ran into Deputies Ike Rogers and Rufe Cannon near Bartlesville. In this fight Jesse Jackson was shot three times. The others were captured. Henry Starr escaped.

It was a close shave. But, undaunted, Starr planned the next big robbery of his career.

He organized another gang of such hard characters as Frank Cheney, Lin Cumplin, Bud Tyler, Hank Watt, a laughing gunman known only as "Happy Jack," and a deadly, smooth-faced youth named Kid Wilson (no relation to the slain deputy), who already had ridden with him in the train robbery at Pryor Creek and had a thousand-dollar reward on his head. They crossed into the Ozarks and camped near Bentonville, Arkansas. Starr rode in alone to case the People's Bank. When he returned, he knew the habits of all its employees, the location of every street, alley, store, house, and vacant lot.

On June 5, 1893, Starr and Cheney drove into town in a buggy, leading their horses behind, and smuggling the gang's rifles under a blanket. Their six-shooters were concealed under their coats. The other five outlaws rode in at intervals, so as not to arouse suspicion. It was 2:30 P.M., the time when, Starr had determined, the most money would be in sight.

They drove past the courthouse square into the alley behind the bank. Quickly the others rode up and dismounted. Happy Jack held the reins of the seven saddled horses while the others snatched their rifles from the buggy and ran to their assigned positions. Watt and Tyler guarded the escape route between the bank and horses. Cumplin stood watch at the bank door. Starr, Wilson, and Cheney darted inside.

Wilson swept the money from the counter. Cheney leaped into the vault. Starr prodded four surprised bank officials and two customers against the wall. Within two minutes Wilson and Cheney had all the loose money stuffed in two sacks— one containing gold and currency, the other $900 in silver— and were ready to go.

It also had been time enough for the people to realize that their bank was being robbed. As the alarm spread, citizens seized pistols and shotguns and opened fire on the guards.

Sheriff Pierce Galbraith was in the county judge's office. A boy dashed in and told him the bank was being held up. He ran for the alley where the gang had left their horses and buggy.

Inside the bank, Starr took the sack of gold and currency and handed the sack of silver to the cashier, giving Wilson and Cheney free hands with their Winchesters. Starr ordered the other captives to leave the bank first.

He intended to march behind them as a screen. But once outside, with a score of citizens shooting at them, it was no more dangerous not to stay with the robbers, and they fled in every direction.

With the cashier still in custody, the gang moved toward their horses. Their guns blazed, and four citizens fell. The cashier was wounded as they forced him along the sidewalk. The act of a courageous young lady, employed as business manager in the office of the Bentonville *Sun,* saved his life.

As the cashier, carrying the sack of silver, passed the office, Miss Maggie Wood bravely reached outside, seized him by

the shoulders, and pulled him headlong into the room. Before
the robbers recovered from surprise, she closed and locked
the door.

There was no time to try to recover the loot. The gunfire
from the street had increased. Sheriff Galbraith had reached
the alley and opened fire on Happy Jack. A drayman coming
up the street fired on Tyler, inflicting a serious wound.
Cumplin, who had stood his ground at the bank door, had
one eye shot out, two bullets through his right arm, and eight
wounds in other parts of his body.

Starr helped him to his horse. Then all mounted and rode
out of town, with lead volleying after them and a score of
citizens in pursuit. The posse followed for several miles, but
the robbers outdistanced them and escaped.

The one sack of money netted the gang $11,000. Starr
divided it among the members and ordered them to split up
for a while. But the Territory got so hot they never united.

Tyler died in bed from his wound. Happy Jack was killed
by marshals two months later. A year afterward they killed
Frank Cheney. Link Cumplin survived his wounds and went
to Alaska, tried to hold up an express messenger, and was
shot to death. Starr and Kid Wilson had vanished.

The night of July 1, 1893, two men and a woman checked
in at the Spaulding House in Colorado Springs and signed
the register "Frank and Mary Jackson" and "John Wilson,"
of Joplin, Missouri. The next morning William Feuerstine, of
Fort Smith, visiting the resort city, stepped into the lobby
and recognized Starr.

Feuerstine reported to Chief of Police Dana. Dana investigated. Jackson was Starr, Mary Jackson his alleged wife, and
John Wilson the notorious Kid. Knowing the desperate character of these men, Dana decided to arrest them separately.

He secreted four officers in a room on South Teton Street and detailed Detective Joe Atkinson to the Spaulding House to keep them in sight. Shortly before noon Starr and Wilson went to the Oppenheimer Brothers store. They purchased fine suits of clothes, gold watches and chains, and invited the Oppenheimers to accompany them to see the sights. They rented a rig, picked up Mrs. Jackson at the Spaulding House, and drove to Manitou, where they spent the day, the detectives watching every move.

They returned at dark. Starr and the woman got out at the Spaulding House, Wilson accompanying the rig to the stable. Later, Starr came down to the hotel office. Learning that the supper hour had passed, he walked two blocks up the street to the Café Royal and sat down to eat.

This was the moment the officers had waited for—the desperadoes had separated. Chief Dana and Captain Gathright leisurely strode into the café and walked past Starr's table. Turning suddenly, they pinioned Starr's arms and wrists. Atkinson and his men rushed in, covering him with pistols, and relieved him of a .45 revolver concealed under his coat.

"Who do you think you've got?" he asked.

"Henry Starr," Dana replied.

"If you hadn't got the drop on me, there would have been some corpses around," Starr said.

Meanwhile, Kid Wilson had taken a street car to Colorado City and entered a house of ill fame. When the landlady opened the door to the room, the officers rushed in, ordered him to throw up his hands, and disarmed him.

A few minutes later another squad arrested the last of the trio, Mrs. Jackson, at the Spaulding House, in bed. Under her pillow was a .38 revolver and $1,460 in greenbacks. In a valise nearby was $500 in gold.

Henry Starr.

Kid Wilson.

She told conflicting stories at first of her relationship with Starr and about the money. She was eighteen and attractive. When told the identity of the two men with her, she became extremely nervous. She was identified as a Joplin girl who had become infatuated with Starr a few weeks before and married him, unaware of his crimes.

Starr and Wilson were released to federal authorities at Fort Smith. Four indictments for robbery and one for murder were returned against Starr. He also was indicted jointly with Kid Wilson for the Pryor Creek robbery. Wilson received twenty-four years.

Starr was sentenced to hang for murder. But he swore he did not know Deputy Wilson nor the character of his mission, and had killed in self-defense. He took a writ to the Supreme Court and obtained a new trial on grounds that the trial court had shown prejudice in instructing the jury.

He was tried again a year later, and again sentenced to hang. He took a second writ to the Supreme Court and was granted another trial. Two years later, in October, 1897, he pleaded guilty to manslaughter and was sentenced to five years at Columbus, Ohio, and to ten years on two robberies for which he had been convicted pending his trial for murder.

During his five years in the United States jail his deportment had been most exemplary. He read much and wrote articles for newspapers about the Indian Territory and the Five Civilized Tribes. Apparently he was a changed man, and friends believed that if restored to civil walks of life he would be a decent citizen.

He promised as much to the President of the United States and the Cherokee National Council, which passed a resolution recommending his pardon. Theodore Roosevelt commuted his sentence to expire January 16, 1904.

Starr returned to the Cherokee Nation. He married an Indian girl, a schoolteacher and a very estimable woman. In May, 1904, he filed for allotments at the Tahlequah land office for himself, his wife, mother, and sister. The family took land in a body near Skiatook.

Starr engaged in the real-estate business in Tulsa. His wife bore him a child, a boy, whom he named after the President who had pardoned him. His life as a peaceful and honorable citizen seemed settled.

Starr always claimed that a disgruntled business rival took a trip to Bentonville, found the old charge of bank robbery pending against him, and prodded Arkansas authorities into asking that he be turned over to them for prosecution. Actually, Bentonville authorities had indicted him and kept the indictment alive through the years he was in prison and after he was pardoned.

The eastern half of Oklahoma was still Indian Territory, and Arkansas could not extradite him. But they kept an eye on him and waited. When Oklahoma became a state in 1907 and elected its first governor, Starr became eligible for extradition, and the Bentonville authorities immediately applied for his custody.

Starr could have gone to the governor and shown how for four years he had been going straight. Despite his long criminal record, he had been blessed with an exceptionally large following of sympathetic and influential friends and admirers, and a battery of lawyers who had won him reversals, dismissals, light sentences, and, finally, his release from prison.

They probably would have prevented his extradition. But the lure of the old life was greater than Starr's desire for business success and respectability. Kid Wilson had returned on parole from prison, and Starr took to the hills to join him. He did not even wait to see whether the governor would allow his extradition. The afternoon of March 19, 1908, he and Wilson entered the State Bank at Hoffman and took $900.

Posses from five counties trailed them north through Jenks, in the oil fields, to Keystone, in the Bigheart Mountains on the Cimarron. Other officers searched for them a few days later in the hills near Nowata and the Kansas line.

Henry and the Kid headed for California. They crossed western Kansas into Colorado. The little bank at Amity looked so easy it seemed a shame to pass it up. In the Colorado mountains they split the loot and separated. No one ever saw Kid Wilson again.

Starr reached Arizona. He thought he was safe there. He wrote a real-estate man in Tulsa to dispose of his allotment and send him the money. He had known the man since childhood and trusted him.

But somehow the Colorado authorities learned Starr's Arizona address. On May 12, 1909, he was arrested at Bouse, northwest of Phoenix, by John A. Simpson, sheriff of Powers County, Colorado, S. W. Fenton, a state officer of Oklahoma, and Wayne Davis, a local deputy sheriff. He was returned to Amity, tried for bank robbery, and sentenced to twenty-five years in the Colorado prison.

At Canon City Starr again was the model prisoner. He was made trusty in charge of a work gang. At nights he studied law, and officials declared he already knew enough to pass the bar. He swore he had enough, and, in vindication of his past, wrote a book entitled *Thrilling Events, Life of Henry Starr.*

He admitted his many lawless acts. But he blamed his start in outlawry on the third-degree methods of deputy marshals who first arrested him. He penned a bitter tirade against society and charged graft in the courts, especially those in Arkansas.

He did not mention the fact that he simply could not resist the call of easy money, nor buy fine clothes and jewelry and love women on a good citizen's wages from 1893.

He failed to convince a discerning public, but seemed adept at convincing those with powers of pardon and parole. On September 24, 1913, he was released by Colorado's governor, providing he never set foot again in Oklahoma.

Starr opened a short-order restaurant at Holly. But people were afraid of him. They referred to him as "the bad man from Oklahoma." Business faltered. Starr's infatuation with the wife of a local merchant complicated matters. She left her husband and child to live with Starr, and Starr left Colorado.

He went to Skiatook to see his son. But his wife had divorced him and taken the child. After that, Starr disappeared.

Colorado listed him as a parole violator. Arkansas still wanted him. Oklahoma officers sought him for bank robbery. But he had vanished completely.

In May, 1914, the first of the worst series of bank robberies in the Southwest occurred in Oklahoma. About two weeks apart, one country bank after another was entered by one or two disguised men, who held up the officials and took the money from vaults and counters.

Officers were unable to get a single clue. Detective agencies whose specialty was bank protection threw up their hands. Then someone mentioned Henry Starr.

"Henry Starr is behind it," they declared.

But where was Starr? There were reports that he had

returned to Arizona, gone to Nevada and California. He had not been seen in Oklahoma.

And still banks were being robbed. Between September 8, 1914, and January 13, 1915, thirteen more were held up and burglarized. The Southwest was shocked. Insurance companies threatened to cancel bank policies, and the Oklahoma legislature moved to pass a hurriedly drawn bill appropriating $15,000 for the capture or death of bank robbers and safe blowers, and empowering the chief executive to place a price on the heads of bandits not to exceed $1,000 in a single case. Governor R. L. Williams immediately issued a proclamation offering $1,000 for the capture of Henry Starr, dead or alive.

The Osage hills provided ideal concealment for criminals of the state. It was impossible to round up a gang once it reached this wild country. It had been the hiding place for Starr years before, and posses and individual man hunters made long scouting trips into the area to collect the reward.

Meanwhile, Henry Starr relaxed in the heart of Tulsa in a five-room bungalow with electric lights, hot and cold running water, bath and telephone, and "Laura Williams," the woman for whom he had violated his parole from the Colorado prison.

At night they took regular joy rides over the paved streets of the city in a new five-passenger automobile Henry kept in a garage in the rear. They patronized the local motion-picture house, where Henry saw enacted upon the silver screen reproductions of thrilling events suggestive of chapters in his own life.

He kept out of sight in the daytime, for just two doors from him lived the sheriff of Tulsa County. Across the street was a church. Next door was one of the city's largest public

schools. Every day hundreds of children played in the outlaw's back yard at recess.

Who would think of looking for him there?

Shortly after nine o'clock Saturday morning, March 27,
1915, seven men rode into Stroud, fourteen miles northeast
of Chandler, the seat of Lincoln County, and tied their horses
south of the First National Bank. Three men went up the
street a block east to the State Bank, and entered. Three
others entered the First National. One man watched the
horses.

Unmasked, with no arms in sight, they aroused no suspicion. Not until they were inside the banks did the town
realize that a double holdup was in progress.

The bandits had entered the State Bank too early. The
time lock could not be operated until 9:45 A.M. They took
$1,600 and a diamond stud from Banker Lee Patrick.

The trio in the First National were more successful, obtaining $4,322. Neither group had difficulty. The bank officials
were surprised.

The three bandits left the side door of the State Bank,
with the officials as hostages. They went around to the alley
and came down to the First National. Here they joined the
second squad, who came from the First National. Marching
the groups of officials and clerks ahead of them, they started
for their horses.

At the first alarm several citizens had armed themselves
with shotguns and rifles. As they left the banks, the bandits
began a promiscuous firing up and down the street to frighten
them to cover. When they reached their horses and released
their hostages, the citizens started after them.

The leader shoved Lee Patrick aside. "Let me take a shot
at that son of a bitch up the street," he snarled. He aimed at

a man thrusting his head from behind a building.

Seventeen-year-old Paul Curry, whose father ran a grocery store, had been in the street when the bandits left the banks, herding their terrorized prisoners. Ducking inside, he grabbed a rifle, ran to the back of the store, and took a position behind some barrels. As the bandit leader aimed at the head up the street, Curry fired.

His bullet struck the bandit in the left thigh below the hip, shattering the legbone, and knocking him down. Curry threw another cartridge into the chamber. The wounded man tried to return his fire.

"Drop that gun, or I'll kill you!" shouted Curry.

The bandit tossed away his weapon. The rest of the gang were riding off, except one. His pockets loaded with silver coins, he had difficulty mounting his horse, excited by the rifle fire. Reaching the saddle, he started back to help his companion when he sighted young Curry with his rifle.

He whirled as the youth fired. The bullet struck him in the neck, shattering his collarbone and left shoulder. As his horse reared, he toppled into the road unconscious, money scattering in every direction. The other bandits escaped to the southeast in the blackjack-timbered hills.

Citizens swarmed into the street around the wounded leader. "Who are you?" they demanded, then they recognized the notorious bandit for whose capture Governor Williams had offered $1,000—Henry Starr.

In his clothing they found $1,100 of the bank money and Lee Patrick's diamond stud. They carried him to a physician's office, and while his wound was being dressed, the second robber was brought in and identified as Lewis Estes of Neosho, Missouri. They were loaded aboard a Frisco express car to Chandler and lodged in the basement jail.

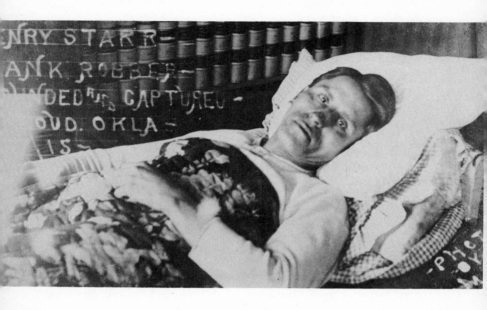

Henry Starr in office at Stroud, Oklahoma, where he was treated for his wounds after being shot by seventeen-year-old Paul Curry following a double bank robbery.

Hundreds of curious people flocked about the courthouse, hoping to get a glimpse of them, while doctors administered anodynes, set broken bones, and redressed ragged wounds. Only a slight huskiness in his deep voice betrayed his pain as Starr calmly answered the questions of officers. For the first time they learned of his Tulsa rendezvous with the woman who, for love of Starr, had left her husband and child in Colorado.

Asked about the robbery of various banks, he admitted some of them. Asked to name his other companions in the Stroud holdups, Starr grinned. He made no answer, and Estes, who listened attentively, but had nothing to say, closed his eyes and pretended to sleep.

Both survived their wounds. They pleaded guilty to conjoint robbery. On August 20 Estes was sentenced to five years and Starr to twenty-five years at hard labor in the Oklahoma state penitentiary.

At Stroud young Paul Curry collected the reward and hundreds of congratulatory telegrams and letters from prominent citizens across the country. His remarkable coolness and courage in capturing the Southwest's most extraordinary bandit was again exemplified when he won the Distinguished Service Decoration for bravery in action in France in 1918.

During these war years Henry Starr again showed his strange knack for getting out of prison. He won the confidence of penitentiary officials, lived up to the rules, and in April, 1919, Governor J. B. A. Robertson granted his parole as soon as the petition reached the state house.

"There's more money in the motion-picture business than in robbing banks," Tulsa friends remarked to Starr after paying twenty-five cents to see May Young in *Sweet Sixteen*. "Ex-waitresses and soda jerkers are getting rich in the movie

Henry Starr's automatic Winchester .35.

game in Los Angeles. It should be a cinch for a famous bandit."

Starr tackled the movies with vigor. A quickly formed company produced his crime-does-not-pay picture depicting the Stroud robberies and Henry's shooting and capture by a boy of seventeen. He made considerable money out of this picture. He was the "Evening Starr" in two more films that followed immediately.

"You have a great opportunity," George Davis, a well-known producer, told Henry. "You get the same amount of thrills out of acting as in robbing banks, without any fear of a pinch."

Starr received a flattering offer from another California motion-picture company to stage a bank robbery for one of their screen plays. The offer also included the statement that they could use him to plan other such robbery scenes for the screen, if successful.

Starr could plan them. In fact, it was believed he had been planning some of his own ever since being paroled.

While making movies at Stroud, he made a trip to Chandler and, by strange coincidence, a Chandler bank was robbed. Later he went to Davenport, and a Davenport bank was robbed.

On February 22, 1921, while considering the California offer, Henry entered the People's National Bank at Harrison, Arkansas, ordered Cashier W. J. Myers to put up his hands and step into the vault. A loaded shotgun stood inside the vault for just such an occasion. Myers seized it and shot Starr to death.

Paul Curry, the boy who captured Starr and Estes.

Bibliography

"A Gunfighter of Old Days." *Illustrated Buffalo Express*, October, 1913.

Barde, Frederick S. (Compiled by) *Life and Adventures of "Billy" Dixon of Adobe Walls, Texas Panhandle.* Co-Operative Publishing Company, Guthrie, Oklahoma, 1914.

Bartlesville Daily Enterprise. March, December, 1908.

Baughman, Theodore. *The Oklahoma Scout.* Homewood Publishing Company, Publishers, Chicago, n. d.

Bell, Major Horace. *Reminiscences of a Ranger.* Yarnell, Caystile and Mathes, Los Angeles, 1881.

Blackwell Times-Record. December, 1896.

Breakenridge, William M. *Helldorado, Bringing the Law to the Mesquite.* Houghton Mifflin Company, Boston and New York, 1928.

Briggs, Harold E. *Frontiers of the Northwest. A History of the Upper Missouri Valley.* D. Appleton-Century Company, Incorporated, New York, 1940.

Buffum, George T. *Smith of Bear City and Other Frontier Sketches.* The Grafton Press, New York, 1906.

Canton, Frank M. *Frontier Trails* (An Autobiography). Houghton Mifflin Company, Boston and New York, 1930.

"Career of Henry Starr, Last of the Spectacular Frontier Bandits." *Tulsa World*, March 29, 1915.

Certain Lands in the Indian Territory. 48th Congress, 2d Session, Senate Ex. Doc. No. 50, January 28, 1885.

Chandler News-Publicist. January, April, June–August, 1915.

Chapman, Berlin Basil. *The Founding of Stillwater. A Case Study in Oklahoma History.* Times Journal Publishing Company, Oklahoma City, Oklahoma, 1948.

Cherokee Advocate. July–August, October, 1893; May, 1894; July, December, 1901; January, September, 1903.

Chisholm, Joe. *Brewery Gulch. Frontier Days of Old Arizona— Last Outpost of the Great Southwest.* The Naylor Company, San Antonio, Texas, 1949.

Cleveland Triangle. March, 1901.

Coblentz, Stanton A. *Villains and Vigilantes. The Story of James King of William and Pioneer Justice in California.* Wilson-Erickson, Incorporated, New York, 1936.

Coleman, William T. *The Lion of the Vigilantes.* The Bobbs-Merrill Company, Indianapolis, 1939.

Connelley, William Elsey. *The Life of Preston B. Plumb, 1837– 1891.* Browne & Howell Company, Chicago, 1913.

Coolidge, Dane. *Fighting Men of the West.* E. P. Dutton and Company, Incorporated, Publishers, New York, 1932.

Cushman, George L. "Abilene, First of the Kansas Cow Towns." *Kansas Historical Quarterly,* Vol. IX, No. 3, August, 1940.

Daily Oklahoma State Capital. June–August, 1893; December, 1896.

Daily Oklahoman. May, 1904; June, 1907; March–April, August, 1915; July, 1919; February, 1921.

David, Robert B. *Malcolm Campbell, Sheriff.* Wyomingana, Incorporated, Casper, Wyoming, 1932.

Dodge, Colonel Richard Irving. *Our Wild Indians.* A. D. Worthington and Company, Hartford, Connecticut, 1883.

Edwards, J. B. "Early Days in Abilene." *Abilene Daily Chronicle,* 1938.

El Reno News. December, 1896.

Foreman, Grant. *A History of Oklahoma.* University of Oklahoma Press, Norman, 1942.

Fort Smith Elevator. January–December, 1893.

Gard, Wayne. *The Chisholm Trail*. University of Oklahoma Press, Norman, 1954.

———. *Frontier Justice*. University of Oklahoma Press, Norman, 1949.

Guthrie Daily Leader. October, 1893; December, 1894.

Harman, S. W. *Hell on the Border. He Hanged Eighty-Eight Men.* The Phoenix Publishing Company, Fort Smith, Arkansas, 1898.

Henry, Stuart. *Conquering the Great American Plains*. E. P. Dutton and Company, Incorporated, New York, 1930.

Henry, Theodore C. "Thomas James Smith of Abilene." *Collections of the Kansas State Historical Society*, Vol. IX, 1905–06.

Hunt, Frazier. *Cap Mossman, Last of the Great Cowmen*. Hastings House, Publishers, New York, 1951.

In re Welty. District Court, District of Kansas, June, 1903.

Indian Chieftain. December, 1892; July, September–November, 1893; May, 1894; September, 1895; January, 1896; October, 1897; January, 1898; April, 1902.

Indian Journal. July, 1902; March, 1908; March, 1915; February, 1921.

Indian-Pioneer History (Foreman Collection). Indian Archives, Oklahoma State Historical Society, Oklahoma City, Vols. 1–106.

Inman, Colonel Henry. *Stories of the Old Santa Fe Trail*. Ramsey, Millett and Hudson, Kansas City, Missouri, 1881.

Jackson, A. P., and Cole, E. C. *Oklahoma! Politically and Topographically Described. History and Guide to the Indian Territory. Biographical Sketches of Capt. David L. Payne, W. L. Couch, Wm. H. Osburn, and Others.* Ramsey, Millet & Hudson, Kansas City, Missouri, 1885.

James, Marquis. *The Raven. The Life Story of Sam Houston*. The Bobbs-Merrill Company, Indianapolis, 1929.

Jenness, Captain George B. "Fight of Payne and the Boomers." *Sturm's Oklahoma Magazine*, Vol. VIII, No. 2, April, 1909.

188 BIBLIOGRAPHY

Lands in the Indian Territory. 46th Congress, 1st Session, Senate Ex. Doc. No. 26, May 26, 1879.

———. 48th Congress, 2d Session, Senate Ex. Doc. No. 54, January 30, 1885.

———. 48th Congress, 1st Session, Senate Ex. Doc. No. 109, February 18, 1884.

Lawson, W. B. *The Indian Outlaw, or Hank Starr, the Log Cabin Bandit.* Frank T. Fries, Orville, Ohio, n. d.

Life of Sam Houston, the Hunter, Patriot, and Statesman of Texas. Keystone Publishing Company, Philadelphia, Pa., 1867.

Litton, Gaston. *History of Oklahoma.* Lewis Historical Publishing Company, Inc., New York, 1957 (4 vols.).

McCoy, Joseph G. *Historic Sketches of the Cattle Trade of the West and Southwest.* Ramsey, Millett and Hudson, Kansas City, 1874.

MacDonald, A. B. (As told by Fred Sutton). *Hands Up! Stories of the Six-Gun Fighters of the West.* The Bobbs-Merrill Company, Indianapolis, 1927.

Marble, A. D. "Oklahoma Boomers' Trials and Troubles." *Sturm's Oklahoma Magazine,* Vol. 6, No. 5, July, 1908.

Mueller, Harold L. "Four Score Years a Fighter." (Life of Chris Madsen). *Daily Oklahoman,* November–December, 1935.

Newsom, J. A. *The Life and Practice of the Wild and Modern Indian.* The Early Days of Oklahoma, Some Thrilling Experiences. The Harlow Publishing Company, Oklahoma City, 1923.

Nix, Evett Dumas (As told to Gordon Hines). *Oklahombres.* Eden Publishing House, St. Louis and Chicago, 1929.

Noble County Sentinel. December, 1896; March, 1901.

Occupation of Indian Territory by White Settlers. 46th Congress, 1st Session, Senate Ex. Doc. No. 20, May 16, 1879.

Oklahoma City Times. September, 1913.

"Oklahoma Outlaw Weds Wealthy Mexican Girl." *Daily Oklahoman,* March 27, 1904.

Oklahoma Red Book. Vol. I (Compiled by Seth K. Corden and W. B. Richards). Oklahoma City, Oklahoma, 1912.

Oklahoma: Yesterday-Today-Tomorrow. (Edited by Lerona Rosamond Morris). Published by Co-Operative Publishing Company, Guthrie, Oklahoma, December, 1930.

Pawnee Dispatch. March, 1901.

Peery, Dan William. "Captain David L. Payne." *The Chronicles of Oklahoma,* Vol. XIII, No. 4, December, 1935.

————. *Oklahoma, A Foreordained Commonwealth. The Chronicles of Oklahoma,* Vol. XIV, No. 1, March, 1936.

Penfield, Thomas. *Western Sheriffs and Marshals.* Grosset and Dunlap, Publishers, New York, 1955.

Personal Recollections and Observations of General Nelson A. Miles. The Werner Company, Chicago and New York, 1896.

Ponca City News. September, 1955.

Powers, Marie Agnes. "Ben Cravens." *Sturm's Oklahoma Magazine,* Vol. X, No. 5, July, 1910.

Raine, William MacLeod. *Guns of the Frontier.* Houghton Mifflin Company, Boston, 1940.

———— and Barnes, Will C. *Cattle.* Doubleday, Doran and Company, Incorporated, Garden City, New York, 1930.

Rainey, George. *The Cherokee Strip.* Co-Operative Publishing Company, Guthrie, Oklahoma, 1933.

Records of the Colorado State Penitentiary, Canon City, Colorado.

Records of the Kansas State Penitentiary, Lansing, Kansas.

Records of the Missouri State Penitentiary, Jefferson City, Missouri.

Records of the Oklahoma State Penitentiary, McAlester, Oklahoma.

Rister, Carl Coke. "Free Land Hunters of the Southern Plains." Part I, *The Chronicles of Oklahoma,* Vol. XXII, No. 4, winter, 1944–45.

————. "Oklahoma, The Land of Promise." Part II, *The Chronicles of Oklahoma*, Vol. XXIII, No. 1, spring, 1945.

Rucker, Alvin. "Amos Chapman, Hero of Buffalo Wallow." *Daily Oklahoman*, April 14, 1929.

Rynning, Captain Thomas H. *Gun Notches. The Life Story of a Cowboy-Soldier*. Frederick A. Stokes Company, New York, 1931.

Shawnee Daily Herald. March, 1908.

Shirley, Glenn. *Law West of Fort Smith. A History of Frontier Justice in the Indian Territory, 1834–1896*. Henry Holt and Company, New York, 1957.

Sonnichsen, C. L. *Billy King's Tombstone. The Private Life of an Arizona Boom Town*. The Caxton Printers, Ltd., Caldwell, Idaho, 1942.

————. *Roy Bean, Law West of the Pecos*. The Macmillan Company, New York, 1943.

Starr v. United States. 153 U. S. 614, May, 1894.

Starr v. United States. 164 U. S. 627, October, 1896.

Stillwater Advance. March, 1901.

Streeter, Floyd Benjamin. *The Kaw. The Heart of a Nation*. Farrar and Rinehart, Incorporated, New York, 1941.

————. *Prairie Trails and Cow Towns*. Chapman and Grimes, Boston, 1936.

Terrill, I. N. "The Boomers' Last Raid." *Sturm's Oklahoma Magazine*, Vol. VIII, No. 2, April, 1909.

Texas, A Guide to the Lone Star State. Compiled by the Workers of the Federal Writers' Program of the Works Projects Administration in the State of Texas. Hastings House, New York, 1940.

Thoburn, Joseph B. *A Standard History of Oklahoma*. The American Historical Society, Chicago and New York, 1916 (5 vols.).

———— and Wright, Muriel H. *Oklahoma, A History of the State and Its People*. Lewis Historical Publishing Company, Inc., New York, 1929 (4 vols.).

Thrilling Events, Life of Henry Starr. Written in the Colorado Penitentiary by Himself. Published July, 1914, and sold by R. D. Gordon, Tulsa, Oklahoma.

Tilghman, Zoe A. *Outlaw Days.* Harlow Publishing Company, Oklahoma City, 1926.

Tragedies of the Osage Hills (As told by the "Sage" of the Osage). The Osage Printery, Pawhuska, Oklahoma, n. d.

Valentine, Alan. *Vigilante Justice.* Reynal and Company, New York, 1956.

Vinita Daily Chieftain. January, September, 1903; May, 1904.

Vinita Leader. January, 1897.

Wellman, Paul I. *The Trampling Herd.* Carrick and Evans, Incorporated, New York, 1939.